Joseph Skipsey

A Book of Miscellaneous Lyrics

Joseph Skipsey

A Book of Miscellaneous Lyrics

ISBN/EAN: 9783744775632

Printed in Europe, USA, Canada, Australia, Japan

Cover: Foto ©Thomas Meinert / pixelio.de

More available books at **www.hansebooks.com**

A BOOK OF

MISCELLANEOUS LYRICS,

BY

JOSEPH SKIPSEY.

AUTHOR OF

"ANNIE LEE," "TWO HAZEL EYES,"
"MEG GOLDLOCKS," "MY MERRY BIRD," "THE FAIRIES ADIEU,"
AND OTHER DITTIES.

———————

BEDLINGTON :

PRINTED FOR THE AUTHOR BY GEORGE RICHARDSON,

1878.

————

To

ROBERT SPENCE WATSON, ESQ.,

SOLICITOR, NEWCASTLE-UPON-TYNE,

AS A TOKEN

OF AFFECTION AND ESTEEM FOR THE MAN,

HIS CULTURE AND HIS PRINCIPLES,

THIS BOOK IS INSCRIBED

BY HIS FRIEND

THE AUTHOR.

Backworth, August, 1878.

PREFACE.

PARTLY from deference to the opinion of a few well-wishers, and partly from an impression that it would be proper so to do, I beg leave to state that the author of the following Lyrics is a coal-miner, and that he was sent into the coal-pits of Percy Main, near North Shields, to help to earn his bread while yet a mere child, and when the sum total of his learning consisted in his ability to read his A.B.C., or at most his A. B. ab card. When it is stated that the require-ments of the times at that period necessitated the young to be in the mines from twelve to fourteen hours per day, it will be seen that they had little leisure for self-culture, and that only by dint of perseverance, and by not allowing the few spare moments to remain un-utilized that should present themselves, could those who had a desire, acquire anything in the shape of education. The author being pos-sessed with the requisite aspiration, soon had felt what is thus expressed, and instead of spending his hours on the play-ground, he devoted his Sundays and other holidays to the acquisition of the ability to read, and to decipher simple arithmetical questions. These operations were usually per-formed in his mother's garret, (he had no father the father having lost his life when the writer was a baby " in arms") whilst he learned himself to write with a piece of chalk on his trap-door—a door connected with the ventilation of the mine, and which it was his duty to attend. In this rude way were his studies pursued, and with what success may be indicated by the fact, that before he was eleven years old, he had formed the romantic notion of trying to commit the Bible to memory, and that he had actually acquired a number of the chapters by "heart," and was only prevented from proceeding further by the redicule of a grey-bearded wiseacre to whom he had had the temerity to disclose his project. By the time he was sixteen years old, he had from a Lindley Murray which had been presented to him by an aunt, and through much effort and perseverance, acquired a knowledge of the elements of English Grammar. Other studies chiefly of a scientific nature succeeded this—then that of poetry—or rather the poetry of celebrated poets, as Shakspere, Milton, and Burns, for otherwise the love of the muses had grown up with him from his infancy, and he had actually practised verse-making, while he was yet a child behind his trap-door.

After the elapse of a few more years, and after making repeated efforts and in vain to get a suitable situation out of the mines, he printed a batch of lyrics (1859), which earned him the respect of several eminent persons in the North of England. Through the kindness of one of these he was placed into the office of sub-store-keeper at The Gateshead Iron Works. This was at the commencement of the year 1859, and at the latter part of the year 1863 he was placed, on the commendation of the same kind friend, as sub-librarian to the Literary and Philosophical Society, Newcastle-upon-Tyne. This latter office, which was certainly extremely congenial to his tastes, he only held a few months, when from the inadequacy of the income to meet his do-

mestic needs he was necessitated to give it up, again to find
himself a toiler in the coal mines. In 1871 he again resort-
ed to the printer, and issued a small volume of poems, which
obtained a kindly notice not only from the *Newcastle Chronicle*
and the rest of the local papers, but also from many of the
London weeklies, including the *Literary World* and the *Sun-
day Times*, and also a kind word from the *Athenæum* and
the *Spectator ;* whilst several of the pieces included in this
issue were honoured by a translation into the French
tongue and published in the *Beautés de la Poësie de Anglaise
par le Chevalier De Chatelain.* The encouragement thus
received has helped to stimulate the author to persevere in
his attempts at self-culture, and the embodiment, when the
impulse has come upon him, of his sentiments and feelings
in verse, until he finds himself in possession of material for
the present book—a book which he now submits to the
public in the hope that it may at once prove of some interest
to the peruser, and be the means of rendering some little
personal benefit to himself.

In conclusion, the author would say, that should the present venture, several of the Pieces of which have already
seen the light, find favour with the public, it may in due
time be succeeded by a companion volume—a book of Songs
and Ditties, and in the two brochures thus offered, would
be comprised nearly the whole of his verse that the author
would care to put into print.

JOSEPH SKIPSEY,

Backworth.

ERRATA.

At page 4—" So thro' life," for ' life " read " strife."
     ,,   21 and 25—for " Io Pean !" read " Io Pæan !"
     ,,   53—for " Did I weep," read " Did I sleep ?"
     ,,   95—for " 1868," read " 1876."
     :,   119—for " hid his voice," read " hid his face."
     ,,   129 —" In vain to point the past," for " past " read " present."
     ,,   167—for " Are the deeds," read " Still are the deeds."

CONTENTS.

———

MISCELLANEOUS LYRICS.

MAN

WHAT IS HE?

WHAT is Man?   The question floweth
   From the lips with ease, and yet
He who best can answer knoweth,
   Answer true were hard to get.
Not the Sphinx in Egypt olden
   Did a deeper question ask;
Love to strengthen and embolden
   Be to answer mine the task!

But a feeble mortal merely,—
   An immortal now believed;
One too complex to be clearly
   Even by himself conceived;
One both complex and immortal,
   Say I inward going, yea,
Death is but to Life the portal,
   As the poets always say.

From the Inner Sun, a sparklet,
    He (Man) glows a star in turn,
From whose life-evolving circlet
    Other living powers are born ;
These again their source enringing,
    To the seeric ken's unfurl'd,
On its way unending winging,
    In the great a lesser world.

Each deep thought and each great action
    Shrined within our inner skies,
To our rapture or distraction,
    Greets us when the Earth-man dies :
There a meteor, or a starlet,
    Burns it while the years take wing ;
To the cheek the guilt-born scarlet,
    Or the glow of bliss to bring.

Empires come and go ; the granite
    Boulder moulders into clay—
From each pathway shall each planet
    And its splendour pass away.
But whilst these away have vanished,
    Not one thought and not one deed,
Tho' awhile to Lethe banished,
    But shall live our worth to meed.

Not our merit or demerit,
  But to crown or punish—ne'er ;
In the regions of the spirit,
  Other ends life's issues bear.
Deeper than the ocean, even,
  Higher than Orion still—
Still to them the power is given,
  On to go for good or ill.

Boundless still for good and evil ;
  Not for good or evil—loth,
Loth were truth to call him devil,
  Man's a god and devil both.
But the devil weakens, stronger
  In his person grows the god,
Till a slave to sin no longer,
  Bright's the pathway by him trod.

Up thro' ill the good still rises,
  And the souls thus risen see
What still hid from dimmer eyes, is
  Without ill no good can be.
Nay thro' strife with the infernal,
  And the sinful only can,
In the courts of the Eternal,
  Be a high seat won by Man.

From the shatter'd limbs of Cælus
  Given to the ocean waves,
Venus rose as legends tell us,
  She whose grace the heart enslaves.
So thro' life with evil shatter'd,
  May we seem a moment when
Lo ! from out the relics scattered
  Springs what's hailed a God to Men.

What is Man ? You have my answer,
  In a may be less prized song,
Than a tip-toed, tight-rope dance, were
  By yon wonder stricken throng.
Yet however faulty seems it,
  From a soul the truth would know,
And for Truth's advantage streams it—
  Would all lauded songs did so.

THE SEER.

Would I could waken numbers, brighter, sweeter,
    Than is the lark's song in the cloud above ;
Then would I tell you in befitting metre,
    How much the Seer is worthy of your love.

Shy, sensitive is he, and far from equal
    Unto the battle of material life ;
He strives unheeded, and too oft the sequel
    Unheeded falleth in the bitter strife.

Averse to falsehood and pretences hollow,
    Averse to slander, cruelty and wrong ;
He scorns the gilded car of pomp to follow,
    And underneath is trampled by the throng.

Too nobly strung of self—to brook the mention—
    Of aught essential to his personal gain—
Too finely strung to pleasure in contention :
    He seeks within the peace he would obtain.

Unlike the crowd who never dare look inward,
    Lest they a hideous spectre there should meet ;
Would point to secret longings prompting sinward,
    He looks within and finds a solace sweet.

There in a conscience pure he sees a charmer,—
    A harper from whose harp such tones are hurl'd ;
They act as mighty spells, as tested armour,
    To shield him from the malice of the world.

" Go on brave heart," he hears an anthem chanted,
    The distant echoes of that harp's weird tones ;
" Go on—to thee a richer dower is granted
    Than that which gilds a hundred monarchs' thrones.

" Thou may'st be thrust aside and scorned and taunted
    As being a lunatic, a knave or fool ;
Thou hast within thy inner being planted
    A power that yet shall put the world to school.

" Thou may'st be destined here to tribulation ;
    Thy every pang shall prove a key by which
Thou shalt unlock some safe of the Creation,
    And with its precious stores thy mind enrich.

" Illumined by that sun forever-burning,
  Deep in the centre of the inner spheres ;
Thou shalt be gifted with the gift of learning,
  What lieth hidden from thy mortal peers.

"In every planet in the midnight heaven,—
  In every hue doth in the rainbow blend,
Shalt thou perceive a lore and meaning, given
  To very few on earth to comprehend.

" The very flower upon the meadow blowing,—
  The very weed down trampled on the road,
Shall be to thee a priceless casquet, glowing
  With glories hinting of the light of God.

" In every breezelet—nay, in the commotion
  Of raging winds—in every streamlet clear,—
Nay, in the roaring of the mighty ocean,
  Shalt thou hear sounds will gladden thee to hear.

" Thus shalt thou in the Universe external,
  The Universe internal read, and so
Possess what shall be to the weal eternal
  Of earth's benighted 'habitants to know.

" Encrowned by knowledge thus and a volition
　　Still to the highest purposes attuned
Shalt thou, a king go forth, and superstition
　　Discrown shalt thou, and with thy glance confound.

" ' Woe ' black-browed guilt shall cry ; and ' woe ' and
　　　vanish
Despair and desolation, sisters sad ;
And for the hydra-brood thou thus shalt banish,
　　Celestial Love shall make the spirit glad.

" Uplifting them by slow, yet sure gradations,
　　From spheres inferne into the spheres superne,
Shalt thou thus prove a boon unto the nations,
　　And in return a boon divine shalt earn.

" If not in monuments of brass or marble,
　　Deep in Mens' spirits shall thy glory glow ;
And little ones shall of the wonders warble
　　Accomplished by the wise man long ago.

" All this and more than this shall be thy guerdon,
　　The sense of having acted right !"—So says
The happy echo of that harp's sweet burden
　　A certain Seraph in his bosom plays.

And this enableth the true seer ever
   To triumph tho' he falleth, and to pray
That theirs like his may be a potion, never,
   Who plot and plan to take his life away.

Ah, to the last his words and deeds are sweeter
   Than is the lark's song in the cloud above ;
And rare the bard could find befitting metre,
   To hymn the love we owe this child of Love !

LO, A FAIRY.

Lo, a fairy on a day
Came and bore my heart away ;
But as she secured her prize,
Sweetest smiles illumed her eyes,
   And, hey lerry, lerry O !

From that moment my career
Lay thro' dells and dingles, where
Pleasure blossom'd out of pain—
Where grief changed her dying strain
   To " hey lerry, lerry O !"

OMEGA.

WRAPT in fancy by a river,
That flows onward ever, ever,
Down I sat me while the moon
In her fairest vesture shone—
All was still as death, when lo!
Down the solemn tide did flow
Fays that once with pleasure thrill'd me,—
Fiends that once with horror chill'd me—
Social Glee and sullen Care,
Lofty Courage, crouching Fear,
And—ah! who with dire Despair?
She on whom my heart has hung,
She who oft my heart has strung,
While the heavy-footed years,
Sought to bury her in cares!
" One by one, and two by two,
They the graceful, they the true,
Went my idols long ago,
And must thou desert me now?"

Thus I frantically cried,
When a look was cast behind,
Clung—shall cling unto my mind,
    And a hollow voice replied ;—
" All things go the way we're going,
    From the quest refrain—
All, all that be—the Earth, the Sea,
Yon Moon above, the Stars that move
In concord o'er yon crystal ;
Yea, all to one vast gulph are flowing,
    And thy cry's in vain ?"

Heard I aright, what is my cry
A cry in vain ? what means reply
So dark as this ? Can earth and sky—
Can all my hope, my pride, my joy,
With earth and sky take wing and fly ?

Can that for which I've daily borne
With insult, empty scoff and scorn,
For which I've labour'd still to earn,
'Till Life itself's a burden grown—
Can that one day from me be flown ?

Can that for which I've inly bled,
And tears of blood, not water shed ;
For which I've lain on thorny bed,

Who else had lain on bed of down—
Can that one day from me be flown?

Can that for which I've wooed disgrace—
Look'd Persecution in the face;
For which I've barter'd pelf and place,
And donn'd instead the martyr's crown—
Can that one day from me be flown?

What can the all my soul held dear,
The soul itself and all whate'er
    Comprised in this Great Universe
Take wing and never more return?
    Can Life itself thus prove a curse,
And mock the mighty souls who yearn
Even to obtain the life superne—
    Sung in prophetic verse?

Forbid it Truth!—"It is forbid!"
Rang in my soul as voice ne'er did,
A voice whose tone the quester chid;—
"It is forbid.   On facts alone
From battle with externals won,
The common understanding may
Persist another thing to say;
But whoso looks Life's surface under

The Veil of Isis seeks to sunder,

And on internals cares to ponder,

Even such a one will find whate'er

Has been will be, tho' Earth's rude sphere

To outer sense should disappear—

Tho' to that sense, above, below,

All things appear to come and go,

Yet to the inner living still

With dread to chill, with bliss to thrill—

To warn, encourage, pain or charm,

To lead to blessedness, or harm ;

To whip or bless us for the act

Another's heart has soothed or racked ;

Yea, all things and all deeds whatever

    Shall to the inner sense remain—

Shall constitute a fountain ever

Of what should nerve for high endeavour—

    Of what, once drank, should heart and brain,

So fire that Man, would rue ah, never !

    That he was born tho' born to pain—

       Thy cry is not in vain."

STANZAS.

The hopes that allured me
To cope with the worst,
At length have secured me
The tortures accurst,
Of fever and grief,
And frenzy—in brief
Ills—ills from which Death is the only relief.

But Titan-like lieth
My soul in her chains—
Hourly she sigheth,
The answer she gains,
But adds night and day
To pain and dismay—
'Tis the scream of the vulture despair at his prey.

LOVE WITHOUT HOPE.

THE glory of her charms I felt,
  And thro' my frame electric ran
What made my stubborn heart to melt,
  And feel as hearts of passion can ?
And from that hour, her eyes of jet,
  And every trait and every hue,
In her delightful being met,
  Pursues me and shall e'er pursue.

A vision bright, a form of light
  She glides before my inner eyes ;
And tho' anear she doth appear,
  In vain for her my bosom sighs—
In vain, in vain, and woe and pain
  Are mine—and woe and pain alone—
Another's arms must fold those charms,
  Which I would give a world to own.

Upon the block with nerve of rock,
  This hour would see my head reclined,
Could such this hour but me assure
  My image in her heart were shrined ;
Yes, yes, for this unequalled bliss,
  Upon the wings of rapture born,
My soul would cleave the air and leave
  Her mortal bonds asunder torn !

A niche possessed within her breast,
  Ay, more than life I'd value that—
What were it then, could I but strain
  Her to my heart my own ? ay, what ?
Entranced I feel, my senses reel,—
  Up in a fiery whirlwind caught
Away, they fly and leave me—ay,
  Half frantic at the very thought !

What would I have, what do I crave,
  What were a sin for me to touch ?—
Yon radiant star that beams from far,
  Her lustre equals twenty such ;
She's past compare a jewel rare,
  Of value more than crowns can boast ;
Whilst I who sigh—ah what am I ?
  A wretch who merits scorn at most.

Far, far above my worth and love
  Is she—and were she less divine,
Another's arms would fold her charms,
  And I were destined still to pine ;
Thus double doomed to be consumed
  By passion's raging fires, I know
On earth a hell as fierce and fell,
  As aught a future state could shew.

Alas ! alas ! we seldom love
  Where love may equal love obtain ;
Our idols in our fancy move—
  Fleet phantoms we may chase in vain ;
We either love what's little worth,
  And live to rue the sequel ; or,
What never can be ours on earth,
  And so must evermore deplore !

THE QUESTION.

WHAT can he ail ? I hear them ask ;
   And what can make his cheek so pale ?
Ah, that to answer were a task
   For which no effort could avail.
To say I love were but to say
   What many another might as well,
Who never felt the cruel sway,
   Which makes my heart with sorrow swell.

Dear are the pains of love and sweet,
   Yet he who loves, and loves in vain,
Endures a torment more complete
   Than any love-unsweeten'd pain,
Nay, keener than the savage fangs,
   Which limb from limb their victim tear,
And much more cruel are the pangs
   Which drive a lover to despair.

With feelings racked, without a spark
  Of hope to give those feelings rest,
The darksome grave is not so dark,
  As is the chäos in his breast.
The brightest hour that comes and goes,
  Might just as well be dull as bright,
His grief o'er all a shadow throws,
  That hides the splendour from his sight.

Unmoved he eyes the sun arise,
  Yea, doth without a thrill behold
The sun down go at ev'ning, tho'
  He settle in a sea of gold.
The sweetest flower of field or bower,
  The brightest star by night revealed,
To him's not rare, nor sweet, nor fair,
  For him no joyous beam can yield.

The tempest swells and roars and yells,
  Up-tears and heaves to earth the oak ;
The death-bolts crash, the lightnings flash,
  And cities wrap in flame and smoke.
Let thunder crash, and lightnings flash,
  And bid him perish as they can ;
The storm he hears, no death-dart bears,
  Like that which makes his life a ban.

O'er all he sees, o'er all he hears,
    The raven shades of woe are cast ;
And all his hopes, delights, and fears,
    Are now but phantoms of the past ;
The past, the present, future—all,
    All now have faded from him—ay,
All save the feeling of a thrall
    He finds he never can destroy.

He wanders wide of human haunts,
    What others do he little recks ;
Their very sympathy or taunts,
    Can little soothe, can little vex ;
Where-e'er he moves, where-e'er he turns,
    One, but one image meets his ken ;
For that he yearns and pines and mourns,
    And yearns and mourns for that in vain.

Away ! away with questions, which
    No mortal yet could answer—nay,
My pangs are far beyond the pitch
    Of seraph-tongue or pen to say ;
To speak of love were but to speak
    Of what another might, whose heart
Was never forced like mine to break,
    Yet while it breaks to hide the smart !

THE INNER CONFLICT.

THRICE " Io Pean !" let me cry,
  And bless the hour that I was born ;
And born thro' love in vain to sigh—
  To cheer my longing heart a morn
Has risen in my ebon sky,
  Such as did ne'er my sky adorn
From out my night of pain—and so
A victor on my way I go.

Transpierced by Amor's arrows long
  I cried—or thought in vain I cried
For surcease to my woe—the strong
  A weakling floundered in the tide.
On which his soul was swept—and Song,
  That still had told my grief, denied
Not only what my pangs had earned,
But e'en the peace for which I yearned.

A tenant of some curse-girt sphere
   Appear'd I—even so—and Pain
Still by a destiny severe,
   Had power my spirit to enchain,
Or to impel his venomed spear
   Up to the hilt in heart and brain ;
And this he did—but this once done,
The measure of his power was run—

Yea, having brooked the worst, I felt
   The power within, with steadfast gaze,
To scan the blows upon me dealt,—
   Life's issues to their cause to trace ;
And whilst I looked, the fogs did melt
   That swathed my ken—and face to face
I stood with Fate's own self and viewed
The secret of the lash I'd rued.

Illumined by an inner light,
   My past a pictured scroll became,
In which my sorrow, my delight,
   My hope, my fear, my pride, my shame,
Assumed a shape and colour quite
   Beyond the power of speech to name—
A chronicle mysterious, man
Engrossed by self might never scan.

Yet gazing on that mystic scroll,
  Enough of its contents was read,
To teach my desolated soul,
  Not all in vain she'd pined and bled
Beneath the lash, the dire control
  Of passions fierce, by beauty fed ;—
Nor yet in vain her longings—if
She read aright this hieroglyph.

As metal by the furnace, so
  The soul by pain is purified
And gifted with a lustre to
  Apparent luckier wights denied :
This was she led to know—and know
  The still more precious truth beside
To gold is turned our dross by pain,
And nothing's lost that could be gain.

Thus learned I from that scroll, and learned
  The way by which to read the chain
Had kept my soul in self inurned :
  Unhappy self that would obtain,
Whatever won is ever mourn'd,
  Whose blessings e'er as bans remain—
Ah would that men would reck this reed,
So would their hearts less often bleed.

With feelings sharpened—eye and ear—
 For others weal I then did learn
To shed the sympathetic tear,
 To wile the frown from temples stern ;
To do the thing desired to cheer,
 To speak the word required to warn ;
And in return a boon did find,
In all appeals to heart and mind.

Ay, with the All-enwoven—both
 The outer and the inner world
Did I survey—e'en in the froth
 By Life's imperious surges hurled
In its unutterable wroth;
 As worthy only to be furl'd
In Limbo's bosom—on Time's sands,
A sheen that seen the soul expands.

That glory in the grass as sung
 By deep-souled bard, and in the flower
A glamour o'er my spirit flung,
 And strove—nor vainly—to re-dower
Her with that bliss from which we sprung,
 When in creation's natal hour
God said " Let there be Light ?"—and up
She leapt enraptured with Life's cup.

Then "Io Pean!" let me cry,
  And bless the hour that I was born,
And born thro' Love to languish—ay,
  To curse that natal hour—a morn
Has risen in my spirit's sky,
  Such as did ne'er that sky adorn
From out my night of pain, and so
A victor on my way I go.

STANZAS.

Alas! the woe the high of heart
  Seem pre-ordained to undergo,
While proud ambition hides the smart,
  And smiles delude the world below.

Their anguish, like a Samson, blind,
  Gropes on in darkness, till at length
It grasps the pillars of the mind,
  And dies a victim to its strength.

E

MUSIC.

I LISTEN to the accents of the silver corded harp,
  And tho' aweary of the darts at me by malice hurl'd,
Aflying goes life's shuttle and aflying woof and warp—
  A renovated soul I seek to renovate the world.

As the spring is to the brooklet bound in winter's icy chain,
  As the shower is to the blossom parch'd by summer's
      hottest breath ;
As sleep is to the body bow'd by toil and rack'd by pain,
  So is music to this heart to whom the jars of life are death.

The bonds in which I'm bound are broken by its magic power
  And the pent up founts of feeling flow in looks and acts
      that please ;
And refreshened as the lily is refreshened by the shower,
  The soul from trouble freed in turn the frame from trouble
      frees.

Nay, not alone from trouble freed—alone by pleasure fill'd—
  Not alone to strength of body and to peace of mind restored;
I'm thrill'd and by a feeling that the ancients may have thrill'd
    When they sang the golden truths and taught what later
      times ignored.

Taught by the glamour under which I labour bright and clear,
  Become to me the darkest legends of an elder day;
And the so-called myths thus said or sung by bards illum-
      ined, wear
    The colours which the True itself and not the False array.

'Tis said that to the Amphionic song, sun-like, up-rose
  The Hundred-Gated City, and howe'er this be I know
At music's touch a tower-girt citadel my spirit glows,
    Thro' whose illumined corridors no hydra-doubt may go.

Not mine to under-go what under-went Arion, yet
  From out a darker sea, the waters of affliction caught,
And on a brighter than a Tenarian shore I'm set
    To marvel at the miracle a melody has wrought.

Not mine Orpheus-like the gift to strike the lyre and chant
  What from another Pluto had another captive charmed:
But mine to know a lesser gift has made despair to grant
    What Pluto's gruesome regions had a place of pleasure
      form'd.

Nay, not a feeler merely but an actor keen am I,
  Empower'd to seize the harp of life and from its cords to
    bring
An anthem such as had compelled Apollo's self to sigh,
  And wrung from him the palm Marsyas tried in vain to
    wring.

Away into the regions of delight and, what is more,
  Away into the regions of the inner life I'm borne
To learn how Nature at one birth both light and music bore,
  And how the planets danced and sung upon Creation's
    morn.

A dream of a lost paradise the Rosicrucians held
  This twin of light and one that light-like points the
    fount superne
From which the glories that enshrine the universes well'd,
  And whence but sprang the soul a spark, a planet to return.

At this the world may laugh and laugh; their jibes are
    spent in vain,—
  I stand above and far above the arrows at me flung :—
So chant I music-fired—and whatever worth my strain,
  For men of brain, not stocks and stones, for men of brain
    'tis sung.

THE MYSTIC LYRE.

HEAVEN-GIFTED was the mortal, thrice-illum'ed by heaven's
    own fire,
  A bard the cords of whose great soul to love and truth
    were strung ;
Who deemed the mighty universe itself a seven-stringed
    lyre
  From which at the Creator's touch the anthem, Life, is
    wrung.

An instrument it is by which a gamut vast is spann'd,
  Whose every tone's in unison with every other tone ;
And which alone is given to the heart to understand
  Who to pity gives an ear of soul—to self an ear of stone.

To such a one the accents of that magic lyre expound
  The kinship of all beings great and small, and how the
    sweet
Yet mighty octave to the key struck in yon planet's found
  Within the little dew-drop that sparkles at our feet.

In the seeming great the little, in the seeming small the great,
    Are render'd by that music to the pure in spirit, plain ;
And the thistle's and the lily's and the mourn'd and envied
    state,
    Are but altos and contraltos in one bright harmonic strain.

In the seeming ill the good is, in the seeming good the ill ;
    But in Life's complex measure what the ill deplored ap-
    pears,
Is often but a needful step into a varied trill
    That terminates with rapture what began 'mid doubts and
    fears.

All height and depth of moral being are compass'd in one
    chant,
    And thro' vast scales descending in the lowest soul is
    heard
True echoes, true, tho' faint, of what the highest soul can
    vaunt,
    Whilst to the lowest full as oft the highest yields a chord.

The measure of the man with all his destiny so vast,
    When the key-note of the living known is stricken may
    be shown,
And the burden of the future and the burden of the past,
    Are but coloured octaves to the note from out the present
    thrown.

The measure of the angel in the measure of the man,
  Yea, he the highest seraph in the lowest serf's conceal'd ;
And the diapason struck on earth compriseth in its span,
  An echo of the heaven itself in angel-states reveal'd.

Not that which was, is that which is, as sang the Hebrew
    sage
  But a duller to a brighter chord ; and that which is, in
    turn,
Is but a stage in life's great march prophetic of a stage
  That awaits the soul's arrival when we leap death's
    dreaded burn.

The mighty universe itself is but a mighty lyre,
  From which at the Creator's touch the anthem, Life, is
    flung ;
And could we heed its music up would leap our souls on fire,
  And up a hymn to Love Eterne would leap from every
    tongue !

SLIGHTED.

Ah me, my heart is like to break,
The envied rose upon my cheek,
The blood red rose is cold and bleak
   Since he has slighted me.

A very shadow lone and pale,
I all unheard my lot bewail,
He listens to another's tale,
   He has no ear for me.

Erewhile as if a toad were I,
He with that other passed me by ;
She " hemm'd " and tossed her head on high,
And he, he scowled at me.

Ah, had he looked upon my grief,
Had he not sought to give relief,
I feel my days below are brief,
   By his harsh ways to me.

I trail about I know not how,
I like a thief slink down the row,
For well behind my back I know,
   The rest all laugh at me.

The one unto the other wink
Whenever down the row I slink ;
Their hearts are filled with glee to think
   How he's deserted me.

The very bairns have caught their words,
As notes are caught by mocking birds ;
By jibes are rent my bosom chords,
   And grief is killing me.

I feel my days on earth are brief—
Ah, could he look upon my grief,
Would he not try to bring relief,
   And rue his wrong to me ?

I dream'd last night to me he came,
A blush was on his cheek for shame ;
He took my hand, he breathed my name,
   He spake kind words to me.

F

Back from mine eyes my locks he drew,
He bound them with a ribbon blue,
He kiss'd me as he used to do—
    He gave such looks to me.

Such looks? No sun will rise or set
When I forget those looks—forget
Those star-bright eyes—those eyes of jet,
    Which stole my heart from me.

The vision fled and I was left
With tear on tear, with heart thrice cleft,
To mourn a lot of hope bereft
    By his false vows to me.

He'll rue that e'er he wrong'd me so,
Yet were my woe a greater woe,
I would not do by him—ah, no !
    As he has done by me.

My heart is rent, my heart is sore,
A canker eats into its core ;
Yet would I breathe my last before
    He'd wring a curse from me.

Alas, alas ! Deceiver say,
How could'st thou wile my heart away,
Then leave me thus by night and day
    To sigh and pine for thee ?

THE VIOLET AND THE ROSE.

THE Violet invited my kiss,—
    I kiss'd it and call'd it my bride ;
" Was ever one slighted like this ?"
    Sighed the Rose as it stood by my side.

My heart ever open to grief,
    To comfort the fair one I turned ;
" Of fickle ones thou art the chief !"
    Frown'd the Violet, and pouted and mourned.

Then to end all disputes, I entwined
    The love-stricken blossoms in one ;
But that instant their beauty declined,
    And I wept for the deed I had done !

PERSECUTED.

LITTLE Anna, cruel elf,
　　Spite of all my reason,
She, she puts me from myself,
　　In and out of season ;
Ah, the imp ! ah, the shrimp !
　　Glee to Mischief wedded ;
Foe to rest—she's a pest,
　　And always to be dreaded !

When I see her bonnie blink,
　　I'm upraised to heaven ;
When upon her ways I think,
　　I'm to limbo driven.
Like the lammie on the lea,
　　Void of harm she seemeth,
All the while on mad pranks, she—
　　Daily, hourly dreameth.

Never goes the sun around,
　　But upon me stealing,
She, she does my soul confound—
　　Sends my reason reeling—
Gars me sing, and while, alack !
　　I in glee am singing,
On me turns, and in a crack,
　　Gives my ear a-wringing !

Pat, she comes and goes—the wasp !—
　　Back anon she hummeth,
'Round my neck her hands to clasp,
　　That to do she cometh ;
So she leads me to suppose,
　　By her air entrancing,
Till I'm twitted by the nose,
　　And again sent dancing !

Ear or nose, or wrung or stung,
　　'Tween a thumb and finger,
How to be avenged now, long
　　Lost in doubt I linger ;
Then when I resolved at last,
　　Rush her pride to humble,
Lo, o'er me a glamour cast,
　　O'er the stools I tumble.

She—the fay !—well-a-day !—
    Nearly drives me frantic ;
Night and day gars me play
    Many a foolish antic ;
Fain would I her presence fly,
    Fain keep at a distance,
But her rein once on, ay then,
    Vain were man's resistance.

Head a-turned, heart a-burned—
    Nay, reduced to cinders—
Nose a-stung, ears a-wrung,
    Shins all sent to flinders !
Pale and thin—bone and skin,
    I'm a spectre merely,
And he who'd play my part might say,
    He'd bought his whistle dearly.

HAUNTED.

LITTLE ANNA young and fair,
  How with heart a-dancing,
I descry her image rare,
  O'er the footway glancing.
Ah, those locks of dusky hue,
  Ah, those eyes that twinkle,
Now I laugh their sheen to view—
  Now my tears down trinkle !

Rare her grace, her bearing rare,
  Meteor-like she glideth ;
And where'er she glideth, there
  Some dire ill betideth.
In the earth or in the air
  Lo, an imp abideth
All, to whelm in despair
  He who love derideth.

So do I—I who love mocked—
　　Feel unto my anguish,
In love's magic fetters locked
　　Night and day I languish;
Not a bit of use am I,
　　Save with arms a-kimbo,
Thus to sit and thus to sigh,
　　And wish myself at limbo.

Oft from tossings to and fro,
　　Bite or sup unheeded
Up, from bed to work I'll go
　　Long before it's needed.
But a-pit, love a-smit,
　　Do all I can do now;
Still a-wry the pick will fly,
　　And no coal will hew, now.

Can it be her voice I hear,
　　When my pick is swinging?
When her tongue attracts the ear,
　　Golden bells are ringing:
Do I dream? or is't her e'en
　　Yonder nook adorning?
Blacker than the coal, their sheen
　　Mocks the coal a-burning.

Daily—hourly, by the elf
  I, who love derided,
Witched—nay lost am to myself,—
  From myself divided:
Lost?—I'm cross'd and tempest toss'd
  On a sea of passion,
And shall so remain while, lo!
  There's a rock to dash on!

Ah, those locks, and ah those eyes!
  Ah, the rest they've broken!
But in vain their victim tries—
  Love can ne'er be spoken:
Man may fathom ocean—say
  The reason of its motion,
But Love's magic never—nay,
  It's deeper than the ocean.

ROSA REA.

The following was suggested by a sweet little lyric, entitled ' Reso-
lution,' translated from the German of Uhland.

THE sun is in the western sky
    And thro' the barley, she—
Comes she, the apple of my eye,
    The rose-cheeked Rosa Rea.

Away I slink the maid to meet,
    As if I went away,—
Alone to please a pair of feet,
    Resolved to go astray.

I whistle as I go, tho' what
    I cannot tell, but know
Right well my heart goes pit-a-pat
    With every note I blow.

Anon, I, silent as the path
    Whereon I tread become,
The power to blow my whistle, hath
    Ta'en wing and left me dumb.

The lark's loud lilt so bright and clear
  Is ringing in the sky ;
A dearer tune I hear—I hear
  Two little feet draw nigh.

Two feet I hear approaching near
  —Abashed I hing my head—
Two little feet a hornpipe beat,
  Or is't my heart instead ?

A floweret I of scarlet dye
  Espy as on I tread ;
The maid who trips this way, hath lips—
  Two lips of richer red.

A floweret I hard by espy,
  A gem of azure hue ;
The maid who hies this way hath eyes—
  Two eyes of sweeter blue.

Those tiny blooms my heart might steal,
  Did not a spell profound
Now gar my mortal reason reel,
  Or gar the world go round.

My senses swim, my sight grows dim,
　A-near, more near her tread ;
Her little feet a hornpipe beat,
　Or is't my heart instead ?

Ah, am I moving on my feet ?
　Or am I on my head ?
Do airy dreams my senses cheat ?
　Am I alive, or dead ?

Not dead ! away, that notion, nay,
　Not in a dream I move ;
Lo, in the clear bright pool I near
　I see my own dear love.

She nears—appears a blink uprears
　My head—O joy !—ah see !
Till night's o'erhead, locked hand in hand,
　Stand I, and—Rosa Rea !

BEREAVED.

One day as I came down by Jarrow,
    Engirt by a crowd on a stone,
A woman sat moaning and sorrow
    Seized all who gave heed to her moan.

"Nay, blame not my sad lamentation,
    But oh, let" she said, "my tears flow,
Nay offer me no consolation—
    I know they are dead down below.

"I heard the dread blast and I darted
    Away on the road to the pit,
Nor stopped till my senses departed,
    And left me the wretch I here sit.

"Ah, thus let me sit," so entreated
    She those who had had her away;
Then yet on the hard granite seated,
    Resumed her lament and did say :—

"My mother, poor body, would harry
Me still with a look sad and pale,
When I had determined to marry
The dimpled-chinn'd lad of the dale.

"Not that she had any objection
To one praised by each and by all;
But ay his lot caused a reflection
That still, still her bosom would gall.

"Nay, blame not my sad lamentation;
My mother sleeps under the yew—
She views not the dire desolation
She dreaded one day I should view.

"Bedabbled with blood are my tresses?
No matter! Unlock not my hand!—
When first I enjoyed his caresses,
Their hue would his praises command.

"He'll never praise more locks nor features,
Nor, when the long day-tide is o'er,
With me view our two happy creatures,
With bat and with ball at the door.

" Nay, chide not. A pair either bolder
    Or better nobody could see :
They passed for a year or two older
    Than what I could prove them to be.

" Their equals for courage and action
    Were not to be found in the place ;
And others might boast of attraction,
    But none had their colour or grace.

" Their feelings were such, tho' when smitten
    By scorn, still their blood would rebel ;
They wept for the little blind kitten
    Our neighbour did drown in the well.

" The same peaceful, calm, and brave bearing,
    Had still been the father's was theirs ;
And now we felt older a-wearing,
    We deemed they'd soon lighten our cares.

" So deemed I last night. On his shoulder
    I hung and beheld them at play :
I dreamed not how soon they must moulder
    Down, down in their cold bed of clay.

" Chide, chide not.   This sad lamentation
    But endeth the burden began,
When to the whole dale's consternation,
    Our second was crushed by the van.

" That dark day the words of my mother
    In all the deep tone which had made
Me like a wind-ridden leaf dother,
    Rang like the dead bell in my head.

" Despair, the grim bird away chidden,
    Would light on the house-top again ;
But still from my husband was hidden
    Each thought that had put him to pain.

" He's pass'd from existence unharried
    By any forbodings of mine ;
Nor till we the lisper had buried,
    E'er pined he.   But then he did pine.

" Down when the dark shadow had falling
    Across the long row gable-end,
He miss'd him when home from his calling,
    With thrice weary bones he would wend.

" No more would his heavy step lighten,
　No more would his hazel eyes glow;
No more would his smutty face brighten
　At sight of the darling.　Ah, no !

" He lived by my bodings unharried,
　But when from his vision and mine,
Away the sweet lisper was carried
　He pined, and long after would pine.

" Ay, truly.—And reason.—The sonsy—
　The bairn with his hair bright and curled,
He still had appeared to our fancy,
　The bonniest bairn in the world.

" As ruddy was he as a cherry,
　With dimple on chin and on cheek ;
And never another as merry
　Was seen to play hide-and-go-seek.

" Yet, yet with his fun and affection,
　His canny bit pranks and his grace,
He wheedled my heart from dejection,
　And put a bright look on my face.

II

" Full oft upon one leg advancing,
　　Across to the door he would go ;
Wheel round on his heel, then go dancing
　　With hop after hop down the row.

" When—Let my hand go !—When he perish'd,
　　The rest were a balm to my woe :
But now, what remains to be cherish'd ?
　　But now, what remains to me now ?

" Barely cold was the pet ere affected
　　By fever they lay one and all ;
But lay not like others neglected ;
　　I slept not to be at their call.

" Day and night, night and day without slumber,
　　I watched till so weary and worn ;
When Death took the gem of the number,
　　I'd barely strength left me to mourn.

" I've mourn'd enough since.　And tho' cruel
　　Mishap like a curs'd hag would find
Her way to my door still, the jewel
　　Has seldom been out of my mind.

" Another so light and so airy
  Ne'er gladden'd a fond mother's sight—
I oft heard her called a wee fairy,
  And heard her so called with delight.

" Whilst others played, by me she tarried,
  —The cherub !—and rumour avers
That now-a-days many are married,
  With not half the sense that was hers.

" A-down on the hearth-rug a-sitting
  The long winter nights she was heard,
The while her sweet fingers were knitting,
  To lilt out her lay like a bird.

" Did I appear cross ?   To me stealing,
  Askance in my face she would keek ;
At which, e'er the victim of feeling,
  I could not but pat her bit cheek.

" Once, when I had pricked this hard finger—
  No he who in grave-clothes first slept ;
No she—with the senses that linger
  I cannot tell which of them—wept.

" She vanished at last.   Ah, an ocean
  Of trouble appeared that black cup,
But what was it all to the potion
  I now am commanded to sup.

" My husband, my birdies, my blossoms !
    Well—well—I am wicked—yes, yes ;
But take my case home to your bosoms,
  And say if your sin would be less ?

" The dear ones to perish thus sudden—
    Not only last night by the hearth—
This morn when resuming their dudden,
    E'en they, the dear bairns, were all mirth.

" Aroused by their voices—a-yearning
  To kiss them I sprang to the floor,
They kissed me and bade me good morning,
  And whistled away from the door.

" Long after away they had hurried,
    Their music a-rang in my ears ;
Then thought I of those we had buried,
  And thought of the jewels with tears.

" Then thought I—what said I—thus thinking
　　Was I, when rat-tat went the pane,
And back into sense again shrinking,
　　I thought of the living again.

" Anon gaining nerve I endeavour'd
　　To open the door, when some-how
The sneck from my fingers was severed,
　　And back into bed I did go.

" Did I sleep. I did weep. To his calling
　　The father had gone hours before,
And now in that havock appalling,
　　He lies with the blossoms I bore.

" Did I sleep. I did weep. Heart-a-weary,
　　How oft have I so wept before ;
Not to weep but to sleep, lone and dreary
　　I've wandered the broken brick floor.

" Did I weep—well, your kind arm and steady
　　My tottering steps, and now you
Go, get out the winding sheets ready,
　　And do what remaineth to do.

" Spread winding sheets—one for the father,
   And two for the darlings, our pride,—
And one for the wife and the mother,
   Ah, soundly she'll sleep by their side !"

THE STARS ARE TWINKLING.

The stars are twinkling in the sky,
   As to the pit I go ;
I think not of the sheen on high,
   But of the gloom below.

Not rest nor peace, but toil and strife,
   Do there the soul enthral ;
And turn the precious cup of life
   Into a cup of gall.

WILLY TO LILY.

Must all the passion which I've strove
    So long to hide be paid with scorn ?
And must a bosom framed for love,
    Be doomed a hopeless love to mourn ?

And must thou still its homage spurn ?
    And must thou still my suit reject ?
And be to me this cruel thorn ?
    Reflect upon the past, reflect !

A time there was and time shall pass
    To me ere that forgotten be,
When side by side from tide to tide
    We played and sported on the lea.

Then, then have I not chased the bee
    From bloom to bloom—oft chased and caught,
And having drawn its sting in glee,
    To thee the little body brought ?

Then, when a bloom of rarer dyes
  Into my busy fingers fell,
To whom was reached the lucky prize ?
  Can not thy recollection tell ?

As oft away as summer went,
  Who pulled with thee the haw, bright, brown
—Brown as thy own bright eyes—and bent
  For thee the richest branches down ?

With blooms I've graced thy yellow hair,
  With berries filled thy lap—thy hand,
—That hand as alabaster fair—
  Had every gift at my command.

Nay, tho' to others dour, yet meek
  I ever was to thee, and kind,
And when we played at hide and seek,
  I hid where thou would'st seek to find.

Upon the play-ground still unmatched
  Was I, unless with thee I played ;
And then it seem'd to those who watched,
  My failures were on purpose made.

As sure as did a race begin,
  The palm was mine unless you joined;
Then strive who might the race to win
  Did I with thee not lag behind?

The ball I knocked to others mocked
  Their efforts to arrest its flight;
But when my ball to thee was knocked,
  Did it not on thy lap alight?

None, up and down so well I bobbed,
  To skip the rope with me would try,
Didst thou attempt? my skill was robbed;
  If others skipped thee out—did I?

The smothered sneers of our compeers,
  Would hint how acts like these were read,
What then? the while was not thy smile
  Upon thy little lover shed?

Time vanished thus and childhood past;
  But ere the lasses reach their teens,
Atween them and the lads a vast
  Mysterious distance intervenes.

I

They seldom on the green appear
    In careless sport and play ; and if
They join the throng erect they wear
    Their head and still their air is stiff—

They ail they know not what.   And such
    The change that on my lassie fell ;
Then would she shrink my hand to touch,
    And I have feared her touch as well.

Had I changed too ? This I can tell,
    That touch o'er me a spell would cast ;
And did I pass her in the dell
    With slow and snail-like pace I pass'd.

Her voice had lost its former ring ;
    Yet in that voice such power was flung,
I better liked to hear her sing
    Than when of old to me she sung.

Her touch, her tone, her sight would gar
    Me shake, and tho' with all my might
I strove to please and please but her,
    I ever blundered in her sight.

When by the hearth she sewing sat,
   Did I to thread her needle try
Still, still my heart played pit-a-pat,
   And still I missed the needle's eye.

Then when I held to her the hank,
   Such slips and knots occurred we heard
Aunt's dreaded tongue go clink and clank,
   Before the dancing end appeared.

" What ails the lass ?" she often said ;
   "She's sound asleep !" once said, and flew
And snatched and snapped the tangled thread ;
   Whilst I, I know not how, withdrew.

Away too fled those hours !—Alack !
   They came and went like visions rare,
To mock the heart, delude, and wrack,
   And leave the gazer in despair.

Ah, less—tho' sun-illum'ed—less fair
   The bubbles dancing down the burn :
And let them burst, they'll re-appear
   Ere those delightsome hours return.

Yet they may live in thought, and could
　　They live in Lily's thought again ;
Would she not change her bearing ? would—
　　Would she not change her bitter strain ?

Would she her Willy still disdain ?
　　Would she continue thus to gall
And put me to this cruel pain ?
　　Recall to mind the past, re-call !

A CRY FOR POLAND.

How long shall injustice prevail ?
　　How long shall the weak rue the strong ?
The children of Poland bewail
　　The yoke of the Russian ?—How long ?

Lo ! one generation goes by,
　　And another succeeds as of old,
Yet no liberation is nigh—
　　Yet theirs are afflictions untold.

The hero, whose lustre and worth,
  Might add to his nation's renown,
Still seeks at a far foreign hearth,
  The shelter denied at his own.

No star left her home to illume,
  The mother heart-broken and lorn—
The mother looks round on her gloom,
  And curses the hour she was born.

In sight of the husband, or sire,
  The wife or the daughter's defiled;
And to quench a demoniac ire,
  Both mercy and love are reviled.

The smoke of the blood of the wise,
  The holy, heroic, and good,
Ascends from the earth to the skies,
  And still crave the blood-hounds for blood.

How long shall injustice prevail?
  And insult, and murder, and wrong,
Cause high-hearted Poland to wail?
  Thou God of the helpless! how long?

MISFORTUNE.

AWAY with the muses of frolic !—away
　With the haunts of diversion and folly !—and mine—
Ay, mine be the joy to awaken a lay,
　And to weave for misfortune a garland divine.

We shrink at life's shadows and fly to the bowl,
　Tho' warned and reminded again and again
That the death of the reason's the death of the soul,
　And what seemeth a loss may in fact be a gain.

Full often to us is the loss or the cross
　What the furnace itself's to the nugget of ore ;
And the more we are freed from mortality's dross,
　The brighter the soul and her glory the more.

The saint is the grander when smitten by woe—
　The sinner excites a sweet thrill in our breast ;
And still from the presence of sorrow shall flow
　What endeareth the spirit by sorrow possesst.

Cleopatra of old threw o'er Cæsar a spell,
  And her life was a chain of such triumphs and yet
To the soul her real glory began when she fell,
  And her blood as a meal to the viper was set.

Not only the victims of virtue we mourn,
  But the victims of error our pity enthral;
And the tear we let fall o'er a Lucretia's urn,
  Leaves a tear o'er the urn of a Helen to fall.

Not alone round the brows of the martyrs of right,
  But a halo encircles the victims of wrong;
And if history's muse in a Hampden delight,
  Not less is a Stuart the idol of song.

Endeared thro' affliction, thro' anguish endeared,
  By pity to many a vigil is kept
Who else, with the idols by fashion revered,
  Unmourned in the waters of Lethe had slept.

The mortal immortal becomes upon earth,
  And the spirit thro' trials is helped to the goal,
Where the mantle of glory and girdle of worth,
  Are the meed that awaiteth the tender in soul.

Be our state e'er so lofty, down we must sink,
　　When the dire wheel of fortune moves on, as it may,
But the greater the blow sooner broken the link
　　By which we are bound to what smacks of the clay.

Then give me the gift to awaken a lay,
　　And to weave for misfortune a garland divine ;
And the world and its follies may go on their way—
　　A rapture unknown to the giddy is mine.

ALL IS VANITY :

Or, THE ASCETIC SAGE.

From pleasure's cup the sage had drank,
　　Till from a surfeit plagued—till lo !
The blossom in his nostril stank,
　　That once had set his heart a-glow.
By duty led he then began
　　To paint the lures in language stern,
That but debase the inner man,
　　And blind him to his weal eterne.

" From all that I have seen or heard
  This world," he said, " is but a show,
And only can the heart afford
  What tends to bitter strife and woe ;
Nay in its clutch, do what we will,
  Upon our erring steps attend
Annoyance and vexation still,
  To cross and wrack us to the end.

" That bubble frail, in sheen unmatched,
  Attracted by its radiance rare,
Do we stretch out our hand to snatch't ?
  The jewel melts into the air :
So will the golden wish we prize
  Seem all but in our fingers locked,
And then evanish from our eyes
  And leave us tantalized and mocked.

" Does glory captivate the soul ?
  Do we for bay or laurel crave ?
And do we seek the distant goal
  Assured the prize is for the brave ?
Years roll away and life is past
  And in the end what at the most,
For sleepless nights and labours vast—
  What have we but a blank to boast ?

K

"To drink we fly in woe, and drunk
　　Is thus what makes us fools—in fact
Down to a lower level sunk,—
　　The brute, in brutal acts, to act ;
Again becoming self-possess'd,
　　What rankles in the bosom—ay
What but a ten times direr pest
　　Than that from which we strove to fly ?

"By beauty's dazzling spells beset,
　　The strong, the weak, the grave, the gay,
On locks of gold, on eyes of jet,
　　May dream the transient hours away ;
May dream to wake, and what ? to learn
　　Those locks are worse than serpents fell ;
Those eyes but fires of hate and scorn
　　Ordained to make our life a hell.

"The supple knee we yield to gold,
　　And seek for happiness in pelf ;
And what's our gain but cares untold ?
　　And what's our loss but manhood's self ?
We lose what gold has never bought,
　　We gain but what degrades the man,
And for the happiness thus sought
　　We yet may find it—when we can.

" Deluded still are we ! and should
    We grasp at last the boon esteemed,
The victim of a ban then would
    We deem it other than we deemed ;
Nay, nay, our idol at the best
    Is e'er a thing defective found,
Which fails to satisfy the breast
    And less will satisfy than wound.

" The strife for gold, the chase of fame,
    Of pleasure's or of beauty's charms,
Subjects the soul to sin and shame,
    And to a thousand lesser harms ;
Then let thy vain endeavour end,
    Its promised blessings let them go,
Unto thy spirit's weal attend—
    This world is but an empty show !"

IÖ PÆAN.

TRIUMPHANT o'er trouble, triumphant o'er pain,
    Triumphant o'er all and thro' all we shall hie,
With the cry "Iö Pæan !" and Echo, the strain,
    From her cave " Iö Pæan !" enraptured shall cry.

The storm may set in and the summer may go,
    But when keenest the cold, and the keener the more,
Will a gleam in the cloud and a bloom in the snow,
    Give a pledge of a glory-girt future in store.

When from the dire Box of Pandora out-sprang
    The " ills of mankind," at the bottom was found
What a sweet panacea for every pang,—
    What should prove a sweet balsam for every wound.

As it was in the myth, so it is in the fact,
    And as long as the world on its axis shall move,
The Parcæ from mortals will never exact
    What a ban, not a boon, in the sequel will prove.

Not only our manfold evils externe,

But the ashes-fill'd apples by error pluck'd, they—

Even they emanate from a fountain superne,

And will prove to be true golden apples one day.

Thro' the regions of Erebus lay the rough road,

By which the brave passed to the fields of the blest,

Yet once having enter'd Jove's envied abode,

The trouble made sweeter the pleasure possesst.

Dragon-watched was the idol of Jason's desire,

Yet a triumph awaited the noble and wise;

And as sure as the faggot but heatens the fire,

As sure did the danger but brighten the prize.

Creation itself from a chaos was born—

So sang the Illumed of the centuries fled;

And Atë herself to an Eros would turn,

If aright the vast drift of existence were read.

Nay, neither the gloom that o'er-shadows our skies

Nor the danger that lies on the path to our goal,

Nor the keenest of pangs need awaken our sighs,

From woe the soul wrings the delight of the soul!

Triumphant o'er trouble, triumphant o'er pain,
Triumphant o'er all and thro' all we shall hie
With the cry " Iö Pæan !" and echo, the strain,
From her cave " Iö Pæan !" enraptured shall cry.

— —

SYMPATHY.

In despite of the cold and the gloom,
To ornament summer's bleak tomb,
Blooms the snowdrop ; and lo! at the sight,
Sad Flora is thrilled with delight,
And exults in the moments to come.

In despite of the sneers of the proud,
To garnish my hope's ebon shroud,
Glows thy tear-drop ; and lo ! I'm possessed
Of Flora's rich feelings, when blest
With the sight of the first of her brood.

But once having granted my fill
Of sympathy's heart-cheering rill,—
Beloved ! refrain, it were base
To sweep yon sweet rose from its vase
That the thistle might blossom at will.

THE RING.

THO' many a moon had roll'd away
   Since Essex at the block had died,
The Queen upon her night-couch lay,
   And o'er his end horrific sighed.

"Oh Essex, oh! my joy and woe
   Did on thy joy and woe depend;
And Essex I was doomed to sigh.
   That day which saw thy dismal end.

"It racks my breast and breaks my rest
   To think how in thy hour of gloom.
Thou didst neglect—I fear reject—
   The means had saved thee from thy doom.

"The ring I gave in moments fled,
   Had'st thou to me that ring but sent,
Thy precious blood had not been shed,
   These bosom chords had not been rent.

" But thou would'st die, and I must sigh,
  Tho' slander dogs the heels of fame,
And would deny the fact that I
  Could ever feel affection's flame.

"They say I'm proud, tho' not aloud—
  It's spoken in a bitter tone ;
Tho' not aloud, they say I'm proud,
  And that my heart's a heart of stone.

" Ah, could the world the veil up-lift—
  These tinsel trappings—and survey
My soul on storm-tost seas adrift,
  How would they start at the display ?

" My tenderness has not come short
  Of hers whose tears had thawed the churl :
I've been the dupe, if not the sport,
  Of passions worthy of a girl.

"And he on whom my hope was built
  Ah, even he, a cruel act !—
Immersed me in a sea of guilt,
  Then left me with a bosom rack'd.

" How could his pride the block have dyed
     With his own crimson drops, before
To me he'd yield, to me his shield,
     From faction's fangs in days of yore.

" How could—but was't his pride so vast
     Upon himself the blow that dealt ?
In agony what if I sigh
     For one who mocked the touch I felt ?

" For one who scorned the royal ire ?
     Despised the feelings of this breast ?
Possess'd me with a base desire,
     To make of me a brothel jest ?

" Awake my soul ! exert thy power—
     Another mine terrific sprung—
Take up thy burden, and this hour
     Be, be it into Lethe flung.

Awake, and—oh !"—thus did she sigh—
     " Thou cruel Essex !"—when her ears
Are startled by a din, and by
     Her side a troubled dame appears.

L

" The Lady Nottingham to-night—
    This hour upon her death-bed lies,
And lying in this woeful plight
    ' Go, bring the Monarch ! ' raves and cries.

" A secret rankles in her soul,
    The which she seems right fain to speak ;
But when she tries her eye-balls roll,
    And heavy sighs the sentence break."

For coach and steed at this with speed
    The Great Eliza calls, and see !
Soon Queen and guard, and coach and steed,
    Away into the darkness flee

Away o'er hills and dales they dart,
    A hare-hound from the leash away !
The birds from out the hedges start
    And fly, confounded with dismay.

Echo awakes her myriad tongues,
    And with the tones of wild despair,
The clang of wheel and hoof prolongs ;
    —Harsh music on the midnight air !

Roods, miles are pass'd, and shouts of " Queen ! "
 Soon thro' a castle's halls are heard
Where you may see a wan dame's mien
 Change at the sound of that dread word.

Yet mark not this you woeful band,
 Who with o'erburden'd feelings watch
That moment when death's clay-cold hand,
 Shall life from her endearment's snatch.

In truth the tear bedims their sight,
 And had concealed the fact, had they
Possessed a light more pure and bright,
 Than what their sickly lamps display.

Too man's but man ; and how-be-it
 The spirit would her task fulfil,
The senses weary and remit
 Their aptness to obey the will.

Three nights have vanished since her end
 Appear'd but on the threshhold ; lo !
A bitter thing to see a friend
 Thus struggling with the common foe.

So feel they, muse they, cry "ah me !"
  Or whisper low, or shake the head,
When nears the mighty Queen, and see !
  The dying riseth on her bed.

The band that binds her hair unties,
  Her hair a-down her shoulders strays ;
A gleam re-lights her sunken eyes,
  And o'er her ghastly features plays.

"Well thou art here," she gasps ; "and well
  With death I've striven to reveal
What, what it racks my soul to tell,
  And doubly racks it to conceal.

"When he who late for treason bled,
  Had let the Spanish feel his sword,
The fame on which his spirit fed,
  Was it not graced by your regard ?

"Then gave you not to him a ring
  Averring, 'If at any time
Thou shalt my frown upon thee bring,
  Show that, and I'll forgive the crime ?

" He took that ring, the period came
    When he did need its magic might ;
He gave it me to give—my shame !—
    It never met his monarch's sight.

" My lord to Essex being a foe,
    Prevailed on me to keep the boon ;
The rest is known."—A moment, lo !
    Her majesty is turned to stone.

Her late flushed cheeks are bleak and blanched,
    Her eyes shoot forth a frantic glare ;
Her lips are writhed, her hands are clenched,
    And in their grasp her up-torn hair.

" Hell and damnation eat thee up—
    The seven vials the prophet saw
Be 't thine " at last she cried, " to sup,
    For this base breach of human law.

" Great God protect me, I am mad—
    This trial is too much for one,
With might until this moment clad
    To trample death and terror down.

" Kingdoms have trembled at my frown,
    Or at my smile have danced for joy ;
But now the star of glory's flown,
    That shone upon the hours gone by.

" Ah, never more ! ah, never more
    Will joy, will peace to me return !"
This said she sank upon the floor,
    And there remained her woes to mourn.

Nor could she be consoled, nor would,
    But rather nursed her mind's distress ;
Till sorrow gave her to her shroud,
    And thus did end the Good Queen Bess.

ARACHNE.

I READ in an old book the myth
Of the Hellenian damsel with
The magic needle, when there fell
On me a power—a mystic spell—
I could not well to others tell.

But all at once my soul was swept
Into a sphere where sorrow kept
Her vigils sad.　There on my ear
Awoke in accents deep, yet clear,
What might in my weak English to
A sympathetic ear thus flow :—

" The guerdon of my heavy sin
Forever thus I toil and spin
The fatal cord, the lash accursed,
By which my heavy woe is nursed."

" From whence this wail ?" I inly asked,
When thro' the gloom I saw unmasked

One, from whose thin wan face and look,
I for the needle-worker took ;
And lifting up my voice I said :—
"And art thou she of whom I've read—
Arachne's self ? No answer made
The image pale, nor turned, nor fled,
Nor into air, thin air dissolved :
But while within my thoughts revolved,
A something on my vision loom'd ;
Tho' what it was might be presumed
Not clearly seen, at least by one,
Still bound to earth by flesh and bone ;
But whatsoe'er it was or meant,
Anon thereon her gaze was bent ;
And this way that, her white hands went,
Whilst to their motion keeping time,
Re-woke upon my ear the chime,
Which might in my weak English to
A sympathetic ear thus flow :—

"The guerdon of my ebon sin,
Forever thus I toil and spin,
The fatal cord, the lash accursed,
By which my heavy woe is nursed.

" The sun and moon, they come and go,
The ocean's waters ebb and flow ;

My baleful star must ever burn,
My swollen tide know no return.

" Woe, woe the day, woe, woe the day
I first did feel that piercing ray,
Beneath whose magic touch, behold,
The rock's converted into gold.

"Ah, from that hour did earth become
To me a glad, a jewell'd home ;
Where-e'er I turned enrapt I viewed,
A living fact the fair and good.

" Where-e'er I turned enrapt I viewed,
A living fact the fair and good,
Which to my spirit's chambers sped,
And with the inner beauty wed.

"As casquets in which gems are shrined,
So from the lustre of my mind,
My body borrowed splendour, till
My presence stood a living will.

" Entranced I took the web and wrought
A vision so with beauty fraught,
The gazer held his breath and crept
Into himself, and smiled and wept.

M

" Delusive tears, delusive smiles,
What were you but the serpent's toils ?—
The nectar sparkling in yon cup,
To writhe the lips that quaff it up ?

" Flushed with success I then did cast,
A scornful glance upon the past ;
And from that moment I began,
A course which ended in this ban.

" The very God within me burns ;
My soul a mortal triumph spurns ;
Not mortals, o'er immortals must
I stride, or perish in the dust.

" Thus frantically cried I, when
Was flashed upon my inner ken
Minerva's might and sheen, and I,—
What was there left me but to die ?

" A meteor in the night, her might
And sheen is flashed upon my sight ;
But as the night by meteor cleft,
My soul again in gloom is left.

" I view the den in which I crawl,
I view what doth my soul appal ;
But ah, ere I my plight can mend,
All hope to me hath found an end.

" And now instead of sylvan ground,
Where grief was lost, where joy was found ;
My path is such each step I take,
Awakes the hissing of the snake.

" My night is still by horrors throng'd,
My day is but that night prolong'd ;
The sun may set, the sun may rise,
No soothing slumber seals my eyes.

" Around, beneath, and over-head,
The finger of the Livine Dread
Has fix'd a curse which see—What's this
Would thus o'er-brim my heart with bliss ?

" Yes, yes my hand that vision traced,
Mine ivory brow with wreaths are graced ;
Aloud my pean's sung, aloud,
And she my rival's head down bowed.

" No, never since the world begun,
Was ever such a triumph won
By mortal or immortal—nay—
I've brook'd the worst an earth-born may.—

" The sun and moon they come and go,
The ocean's waters ebb and flow,
My baleful star must ever burn,
My swollen tide know no return.

" And, such the guerdon of my sin
Thus, thus to toil, and thus to spin
The fatal cord, the lash accursed,
By which my heavy woe is nursed."

Thus mourned the damsel; while she mourn'd,
Back into sense my soul return'd;
At which receded from my ken
The needle-worker's image, when
I wept heart-rent, and felt distrest,
Till thro' the chaös in my breast
Did break a light by which I saw,
That thro' the working of a law
Inwoven with our being, we
Can never brook but should be—

Can never brook, have never borne,
But what is for our weal eterne :
That furthermore this maid of old,
Tho' cast in a diviner mould,
Lack'd that by which we only can
—A knowledge of the inner man—
Become by wisdom blest, and so,
In the deep shades of Long Ago,
Erred as to her own gifts—their reach—
Erred as to what all gifts should teach ;
How much to Him—the All in All—
In whom we live and move, and shall ;
How much to Him—to me or you,
How very small the credit due
For any gift we vaunt.   In this,
Arachne her way did miss,
And so incurred what all incur,
Who in life's mystic maze thus err—
The doom her errors to deplore ;
The doom should tear the veil aside,
Did from herself her failings hide,
And gift her with the needed light
By which to know herself aright ;—
The doom should show to her how vain
And weak is man, and must remain

Compared with gods who eras long,
Have scanned the lines of right and wrong ;
The doom by which she in the end,
Would to the Inner Circle wend,
Where crowned with bliss, with glory crown'd,
A nobler labour should be found
To claim her cure than that which claim'd,
When she in Greece with pride was named :
And when the best were foremost found,
To honour her whose genius framed,
What their own triumphs shamed.

"GET UP !"

"GET UP !" the caller calls, "Get up !"
   And in the dead of night,
To win the bairns their bite and sup,
   I rise a weary wight.

My flannel dudden donn'd, thrice o'er
   My birds are kiss'd, and then
I with a whistle shut the door
   I may not ope again.

THE ANGEL MOTHER.

I HAD a vision of the dear departed,
　The while stone-dead to outer things I lay ;
And "Go," she said—"and tell the broken-hearted,
　What now my will shall to thy mind convey.

"I've pass'd the portals I so often dreaded,
　And by the fiery trial unconsumed
I find myself to life, not death, yet wedded—
　Even I whose relics you beheld entombed.

"The body's perished, but the spirit's risen,
　And in a body beautifuller far
Than that which was its cradle and its prison,
　And now is number'd with the things that were.

"To me the baubles of the world have vanished,
　Even with the garments I behind have left ;
But not one treasure from my heart is vanished,
　Not of one golden hope am I bereft.

" The self-same spirit, nay, the self-same being
   In every human faculty the same,
Save with a clearer, keener sense of seeing
   What path to glory leads, and what to shame.

" The wife's devotion and affection tender,—
   The mother's sweet solicitude and all
That did our home a thing of beauty render,
   Is mine, or haunts me still, and ever shall.

" Even from my sphere beyond your sphere located,
   I'm oft permitted to return—to wind
My way through halls my change left desolated,
   A blessing to the dear ones left behind.

" I see the brave man by the hearth-stone sitting,
   To whom my being was and yet is wed,
And while the past before his gaze is flitting,
   I see the tear-drops for his lost one shed.

" Not void of hope the dust he saw enshrouded,
   Itself was but a shroud unto a soul,
Whose vision never could by death be clouded—
   He yet hath sorrows he may not control.

Full often o'er the welkin of his vision
    I see an ebon cloudlet stealing, when
A sigh is utter'd lest his hope, elysian,
    Is but a phantom of the minds of men.

"Upon my knees, unseen, before him kneeling
    I gaze into those eyes tear-blinded, till
A sense of sadness yieldeth to a feeling
    As sweet as ever did a bosom thrill.

"I point the images of those yet living,
    —Thus speak I still as I when with you spake—
When from the past into the present driven,
    His heart is up and toiling for their sake.

"'Even for my girl,' he cries, 'so bright and airy,—
    Even for my little boy just lisping, I
Must try this death-bell monotone to vary,
    And on life's harp awake life's battle cry.'

"As he resolveth even so he doeth,
    And all the little I can do, I do ;
To realize the object he pursueth,
    Or open vistas brighter to his view.

" I cannot wash as wont our jewels faces,—
    I cannot comb as wont their golden hair ;
But I can lock them in my fond embraces,
    And I can gild their minds with fancies rare.

" I cannot fetch the lisper sweet his rattle,
    Nor for the other the piano ring ;
But I can aid my boy-child in his prattle,
    And I can prompt my girl-child how to sing.

" I cannot lead them to the daisied meadows,
    But I can over-look them when they're there ;
And give a golden glow to passing shadows,
    And make the fair sunshine to them more fair.

" I cannot give them gruel in the even,
    Nor on the morn to them their toast convey ;
But when they kneel before the Lord of heaven,
    Them I can prompt for what and how to pray.

" Ay, tho' they cannot see or hear me, ever
    Into the soul of babe and father flows
The presence of their mourn'd one like a river,
    That wakens music where-so-e'er it goes.

" So, as by those the idols of my bosom,—

    Touch'd by the carol of the unseen bird;

Touch'd by the perfume of the unseen blossom,

    The hearts of others to their depths are stirr'd.

" Nay, by each spirit sweet with whom my spirit

    In state harmonic moved and breathed, I'm felt ;

And still alive to every form of merit,

    Still dwells my love with those with whom it dwelt.

" Alive to these—to each high aspiration—

    To every base-born passion yet alive ;

To all that tendeth to man's elevation,—

    To all that downward doth the spirit drive.

" Alive to all most worthy to be cherish'd,

    Alive to all should most excite our dread ;

And being thus albeit the body's perish'd,

    How can it be averr'd that I am dead ?"

FREEDOM.

Would I could to freedom awaken a song
　　Half worthy the theme, then, a song would be sung
Would be echoed on high by the seraphic throng,
　　And re-echoed on earth till with rapture earth rung.

I would tell of the glory she gives to the soul—
　　I would tell of the manifold gifts and the grace
She confers upon those who durst spurn a control
　　That our honour would stain and our manhood deface.

I would tell of the bearing she gives—I would tell
　　Of the truth in the forehead expansive reveal'd ;
Of the tones which ring out like the tones of a bell,
　　Of the smiles in whose dimples no fraud is conceal'd.

Of the manifold griefs she's endured since the morn
　　Man emerged into being, I'd tell—of the pain—
Ay, the deaths out of which she has risen to scorn
　　The demons who labour her limbs to enchain.

As from its own ashes the mythic bird sprang,
　So oft from the dust has she sprung, and will spring,
Ere she suffers or ever can suffer the pang
　That would yield her dark foemen a triumph to sing.

Not dead is she found when her foes deem her dead,
　But, like the blest spirit she thrills and adorns,
She never can die, never sleep on death's bed,
　Whilst a star in the dome of the universe burns.

Of the worth of her children I'd tell, and the weird
　And wild music that's felt in the sound of each name
Of the heroes who bow to her mandates revered;
　Of the souls who have battled to shield her from shame.

On the pinions of rapture a legion would come
　Of the shades of the brave, yea, and hark with delight,
Whilst I sang of a high-hearted Gracchus of Rome,
　An Erin's loved Emmet, an Albion's Bright.

I would chant of the glory that vested the Queen,
　Even Bonduca's self—and Caractacus too—
The sheen of whose souls o'er their fall threw a sheen,
　That into the shade their foes victories threw.

The name of the Maid of Orleans should be heard,
　　To the shame and the glory of down-trodden Gaul,—
The God-inspired Seeress whose will was a sword,
　　Which severed the spell had long held her in thrall.

To the Greek Leonidas the lion-nerved king—
　　To Rome's Cincinnatus and he, his last peer,
Garibaldi himself then a pæan would ring,
　　The sternest oppressor would tremble to hear.

Nor unsung would'st thou be noble Washington, thou,
　　Thou, whose name should be written in letters of gold ;
Nay, priest-ridden Spain would in ecstasy glow,
　　Whilst the deeds of the Maiden of Seville were told.

All this would I do could I sate my desire,
　　But alas, I must leave what I feel is a want,
To a mightier bard and a richer toned lyre ;
　　But where's now the bard Freedom's anthem to chant ?

Where, where is a Milton, a Shelley, and where
　　Is a Burns or a Byron ? where ? Woe is me !
We are mealy-mouthed men without courage to dare
　　What becomes Freedom's children to do and to be.

LET ENGLAND BEWARE.

The following appeared in the "Newcastle Weekly Chronicle,"
November 18th, 1868.

Let England beware, ere for war she declare,
  She incur not the mark of the beast—
That she march not her power the State to secure
  Of the blood-imbued wolf of the East;
It might be her gain that State to maintain—
  It might serve a purpose—it might—
But, if so, let her ask, how much nobler the task
  To battle for God and the Right !

The Bulgarians—they and the Servians may
  Have their faults and their failings—what then ?
They are men, are they not ? and if so, we are taught
  By our feelings what men owe to men :
'Neath their dark doom they cry, and their voice from on
    high,
  Wrings an answer that nerves for the fight—
Nay, Europe is thrilled, and her children have willed
  To battle for God and the Right !

Such horrific crimes belong to past times—
    And the coldest and hardest heart bleeds,
And a blush for our race paints with crimson each face
    When we think of the Turk and his deeds :
Too awful are they for relation, nor may
    Men know them and know a respite
To their heart-pangs till they have resolved for the fray,
    And battle for God and the Right !

An unbounded thirst for lucre accurst
    Must the down-trodden sate—even so—
And in this should they fail they are destined to wail
    The merciless scourge of the foe :
On stakes will the Turk fix his victim and work
    Him such anguish and woe, at the sight
The veriest serf grasps his sabre, resolved
    To battle for God and the Right !

See ! those dearer than life, the daughter and wife,
    A prey to the torturer's lust,
And the Rayah heart-torn, and yet ridiculed, mourn
    His losses 'mid ashes and dust ?
With his dear home despoiled, and his dear ones defiled,
    And a wreck what was once his delight,
What wonder if he in delirium should flee
    To battle for God and the Right !

The temple is burned and the altar's o'erturned,
   And with blood the street runnelets run ;
And the prey-bird and beast hie in legions to feast
  ..On the corpses that rot in the sun.
And the ban-dog's harsh tones, as he crashes the bones,
   Strike the wayfaring man in the night
With a deep sense of dread, while a voice from the dead
   Seems to cry, "Arm for God and the Right !"

For God and the Right, the Revolted States fight,
   And whatever the sequel and end,
If thou too must fight—fight for God and the Right,
   And God shall in turn be thy friend :
The gold-kings may shrink at the dictum, but think,
   Yea, hold-to thy duty, and smite—
Smite the cold-blooded Turk till he find higher work,
   Than to battle 'gainst God and the Right.

NIL DESPERANDUM.

WHY thus mourn o'er star-hopes faded?
  They are only from thy ken,
By a passing vapour shaded,
  And will soon appear again :
Would thou prove a moral warrior,
  Up, and make the present thine !
Trust me every doubt's a barrier
  To life's heritage divine.

Not the Cytherean, truly
  Vain its pursuit and unwise ;
But the joy Uranian duly
  Seek we that, and rich the prize :
But for that be our endeavour
  And, afar our doubt and fear,
We shall be a loser never,
  Tho' a loser we appear.

Tho' by many foes encircled
   Is the outer life, the worst,
By whose shadow life is darkled,
   In the heart is hatched and nursed :
All the ill to man else render'd,
   Is a jest of merry elf,
When compared to what's engender'd
   Thro' the sense-born syren self.

From our bosom the infernal—
   All that's mean, and low, and base,
Every wish and longing carnal,
   Chase we then or seek to chase ;
Clearer to us then, and clearer
   Would life's complex riddle seem,
And our vanished Edens nearer
   Than at present we may deem.

Then would in our bosom clearly,
   Tho' in miniature be seen,
Not the lifeless image merely,
   But the God in all his sheen ;
Yea, we'd there, stamped with the Ego
   Of the All in All unworn
Thro' time's Alpha and Omega,
   Find the best of all we mourn.

Lose we may the husk, and perish
　　What the outer senses prize—
What the inner love and cherish,
　　Never from us fades nor flies;
Hid it may be from the spirit,
　　Only for awhile it's hid,
And one day will gift our merit
　　With a joy to sense forbid.

One with the Eternal ever,
　　Even thus to man's reveal'd,
Time from him his hopes may sever,—
　　Time at last to him must yield;
Let but this be comprehended,
　　Death to our despair were dealt,
And our selfish murmurs ended,
　　Sweet the thrill within us felt.

Glory-dowered the task before us
　　Then would cease to be a task;
Nay, we'd have what could secure us
　　Whatsoever we would ask;
Should a thorn then pierce our bosom,
　　E'en before the pang had flown—
Even that would bloom a blossom,
　　Our right royal heads to crown.

" Valor's born from self-denial,
    Wisdom from each stern rebuke,
Power from every pain and trial,
    That the human soul may brook ;"
This, or anthem more impassion'd,
    Would express the faith we'd hold,
And for us a girth be fashion'd,
    Richer than a girth of gold.

Smiles would leap to hail us victor,
    From each flower and running brook,
Beauty would herself impicture
    On whatever we might look ;
Stars, the blessed stars my brother,
    Would attend us in the night,
And creation's self be other
    Than it seems to common sight.

Would'st thou prove a moral warrior
    Up and make the present thine !
Trust me every doubt's a barrier,
    To life's heritage divine ;
Sagest heroes, heroic sages,
    So have taught since time began ;
Up and earn a hero's wages,
    Up, then up ! and be a man.

THE THOUGHT TOILER.

A THOUGHT TOILER faint and o'er-come by his labours,
And the manifold troubles by which he was girt,
Combined with the titters and sneers of his neighbours,
Lost heart and thus vented the pangs of his heart :—

" I'm a-weary with care, I'm a-weary with care,
Surrounded with woes that no mortal can bear,
Whilst I gaze on the night of my ills and survey,
Not a star to direct my lorn soul on her way.

" I'm shorn of my strength and the few are my years,
The winter of life on my aspect appears ;
Ay, the feeling of death steals apace round my core,
Like the sea-waves around yon lone rock on the shore."

So rang the wild wail when a voice from the spheres,
Where dwell the good angels awoke on his ears —
" Refrain from thy tears, from thy sorrows refrain,
The gloom that engirts thee shall vanish again.

"Tho' in shadows the car of thy destiny's driven,
And thy hopes are extinguished, thy bosom-cords riven,
Not, not in one battle for right hast thou striven,
Unwitness'd by God and the angels of heaven.

"And could but thy eyes now be open'd as they
Will be open'd and not in a far distant day,
Thou would'st see for thy trials a guerdon more bright
Than the jewels that garnish the mantle of night.

" For the lava of thought that has sparkled and burned,
In thy inner-most soul's to a diadem turned ;
And every tear thou hast shed is a gem,
That enhances the worth of that rare diadem.

"And every sigh thou hast breathed to a tone
Far sweeter than music on waters has grown;
And that music will flow in thy new-opened ears,
With a might that shall lead thee to bless the past years,

" Ah then shalt thou see not in vain hast thou wept ;
Not in vain hast thou laboured whilst others have slept ;
Not in vain hast thou sorrowed whilst others entranced
With the pleasures that perish have giggled and danced.

" And every trouble and every burden,
    And every pang thou hast felt and endured,
Shalt thou find," cried the voice, " has its own precious
        guerdon !"
And the Toiler at this to his strength was restored.

A FACT.

Now Gladstone's party bears the bell,
    And now Disraeli's—now
The people really cannot tell,
    For whom their hands to show.

Now this way, la, now that inclined,
    A giddy vane they go,
The victim of each puff of wind
    The demagogues may blow.

1868.

THISTLE AND NETTLE.

'TWAS on a night, with sleet and snow
   From out the north a tempest blew,
When Thistle to her cot did go
   The little Nettle's self to woo.

His errand known, she, with a frown,
   Up from a sock a-knitting sprung ;
Down took the broom and swept the room,
   While like a bell her clapper rung.

" Have I not seen enough to be
   Convinced for ever soon or late
The maid shall rue the moment she
   Attendeth to a wooer's prate ?

" How long ago since Phemie Hay
   To Harry at the Mill fell wrong ?
How long since Hall a prank did play
   Shall e'er be rued by Ellen Strong ?
P

" How long ago since Adam Smith
    Wooed Annie on the Moor, and left
The lassie with a stain ? yea, with
    A heart of every hope bereft ?

" But what need instant cases ? lo !
    Have I not heard thee chaunt the lay
' The fraud of men was ever so
    Since summer first was leafy ?' eh ?

" When men are to be trusted, then,
    —But never may that time befall;
Of five times five-and-twenty men,
    There's barely five are men at all.

" Before the timmed maid they'll fall,
    And smile and weep and sigh and sue ;
Till once they get her in their thrall,
    And then she's doomed her lot to rue.

" For her a subtle snare they weave,
    And when the bonny bird is theirs,
Then, then they giggle in their sleeve ;
    Then, then they laugh at all her fears.

" Another western wind, they woo
　　The bloom its treasures to unfold ;
Extracts its wealth—their way pursue,
　　And leaves her pining on the wold.

" —When men are men, come woo me then—
　　Till then, lo I am on my guard,
And he the loon that brings me down,
　　He, he'll be pardoned on my word ! "

Thus for an hour her tongue was heard,
　　By this, her words grown faint and few ;
She raised the broom at every word,
　　And thumped the floor to prove it true.

In ardent words the youth replied :—
　　" Dread hollow-heart guile thou must,
But deem not all of honour void
　　Nor punish all with thy mistrust.

" A few, not all the lash have earn'd,
　　Let but that few be lashed.　Nay, sure,
The world were topsy-turvy turned,
　　Did not some sense of right endure.

" Destroy the wood, but spare the flower ;
   Consume the chaff but keep the grain ;
Nor harry one who'd die before
   He'd give thy little finger pain."

On hearing this, she sat her down,
   Took up her needle-work again,
And tho' she strove to wear a frown,
   Made answer in a milder strain.

" Forego thy quest.   Deceitful words
   May be, as they have been, may be
A fatal lure to lighter birds,
   They'll never prove the like to me.

" Still by my chastity I vow
   As I have kept the cheat at bay,
So, should I keep my senses, so
   I'll keep him till my dying day.

" The best that man can do or say,
   The love of gold or rubies rare,
Not all that wealth can furnish, may
   Once lure to leave me in a snare.

"So end thy quest." He only prest
　His ardent suit the more, while she
At every word he uttered, garr'd
　Her fleeing needles faster flee.

" My quest by honour's justified ;
　I long have eyed and found thee still
The maid I'd like to be my bride ;
　Would I could say the maid that will.

" Hadst thou but been a daffodil
　That with the breezes sport and play
For all thy suitor valued, still
　Thou so hadst danced thy life away.

" But thou so fair art chaste." Thus he
　Unto her answer answers e'er,
And that too in a way that she
　Must will or nill his answer hear.

And then a chair he'd ta'en, his chair
　Unto her chair he nearer drew ;
Recurr'd to memories sweet and rare,
　And in a softer key did woo.

He spake of moments vanished, when
  The happiest pair of all the young
They hand in hand a-down the glen
  Together sported, danced and sung.

The linnet's self the boughs among,
  The lammie skipping o'er the way,
Sang not than they, a sweeter song,
  Played not a merrier prank than they.

" Ah, these were golden times !"   Thus goes
  His descant till her brow grows sleek,
Till lo ! the lily drives the rose.
  The rose the lily from her cheek.

And now the iron sparking hot
  Around with might and main he swings,
And down upon the proper spot
  With bang on bang the hammer brings.

" Be, be my suit but undenied,
  And ere the moon is on the wane
A knot shall by the priest be tied,
  The priest shall never loose again.

" In heart and hand excelled by none,
　　Henceforth I'd front the ills of life,
And every victory I won
　　Should be a jewel for my wife.

" So should the people of the dell
　　When they convened to gossip say,
For harmony we bore the bell,
　　And bore it with a grace away.

" Nay, lift thy head, be not ashamed
　　If thus to feel—and thus—and, O !
As matters sinful might be blamed—
　　Then saints were sinners long ago."

Here silence deep ensued.　The cat
　　That lately to the nook had stept
To mark the sequel of their chat,
　　Came forth, lay on the hearth, and slept.

The needles that flew here and there,
　　And in their glee had sought to vie
A moon-beam dance upon the mere,
　　Neglected on her apron lie.

In concord with the storm within,
　The storm without forbears to blow ;
And 'tween the sailing clouds begin
　The joyous stars to come and go.

O'er all delight prevails.   Nor swayed
　By doubt and dread she longer seems,
But on our hero's bosom laid
　The maid a dream of rapture dreams.

Dream on blest maid !   An hour like this
　Annuls an age of care and strife,
And turns into a drop of bliss
　The bitter cup of human life.

The tear is by a halo gilt,
　The thorns of life are changed to flowers ;
The dirge into a merry lilt,
　When love return'd for love is ours.

And so our heroine felt.   In soft
　Sweet tones, at length her accents flow—
"I've heard of honied tongues full oft,
　But never felt their force till now.

"Still would I fume as day by day
    I've seen our damsels bought and sold
By some I'd scorn'd to own, had they
    Outweighed their very weight in gold.

"My hour of triumph's o'er.   In vain
    Did I my fellow maids abuse,
I've snatched the cup and drank the bane
    That sets me in their very shoes.

"That turns a heart of adamant
    To pliant wax ; and in my turn
Subjects me to the bitter taunt
    The vanquish'd victor's ever borne.

"That leaveth Nettle satisfied
    To leave her kith and kin, and by
Her ever faithful Thistle's side
    To shelter till the day they die."

THE HARTLEY CALAMITY.

THE Hartley men are noble, and
    Ye'll hear a tale of woe ;
I'll tell the doom of the Hartley men—
    The year of sixty-two.

'Twas on a Thursday morning, on
    The first month of the year,
When there befell the thing that well
    May rend the heart to hear.

Ere chanticleer with music rare
    Awakes the old homestead,
The Hartley men are up and off
    To earn their daily bread.

On, on they toil ; with heat they broil,
    And streams of sweat still glue
The stour unto their skins, till they
    Are black as that they hew.

Now to and fro, the putters go
    The waggons to and fro,
And echoes clang of wheel and hoof
    Within the mine below.

The din and strife of human life
    Awake in "wall" and "borde,"
When, lo ! a shock is felt which makes
    Each human heart-beat heard.

Each bosom thuds, as each his duds
    He snatches and away,
And to the shaft in terror flees
    With all the speed he may.

Each, all, they flee—by two—by three
    They seek the shaft, to seek
An answer in each other's face,
    To what they may not speak.

"Are we entombed?" they seem to ask,
    "The shaft is closed, and no
Escape have we to God's bright day
    From out the night below."

So stand in pain the Hartley men,
　And o'er them swiftly comes
The memory of home and all
　That links us to our homes.

Despair at length renews their strength,
　And they the shaft must clear ;
And soon the sound of mall and pick
　Half drowns the voice of fear.

And hark ! to the blow of the mall below
　Do sounds above reply ?
Hurra, hurra, for the Hartley men,
　For now their rescue's nigh.

Their rescue nigh ?   The sounds of joy
　And hope have ceased, and ere
A breath is drawn a rumble's heard
　Re-drives them to despair.

Together, now behold them bow ;
　Their burden'd souls unload
In cries that never rise in vain
　Unto the living God.

Whilst yet they kneel, again they feel
  Their strength renew'd—again
The swing and the ring of the mall attests
  The might of the Hartley men.

And hark ! to the blow of the mall below
  Do sounds above reply ?
Hurra, hurra, for the Hartley men
  For now their rescue's nigh.

But lo ! yon light, erewhile so bright
  No longer lights the scene ;
A cloud of mist yon light hath kiss'd,
  And shorn it of its sheen.

A cloud of mist yon light hath kiss'd,
  See ! how along it steals,
Till one by one the lights are smote,
  And deep the gloom prevails.

" O, father, till the shaft is rid
  Close, close beside me keep ;
My eye-lids are together glued,
  And I   and I—must sleep."

" Sleep, darling, sleep, and I will keep
    Close by—heigh-ho !"—To keep
Himself awake the father strives ;
    But he—he too—must sleep.

" O, brother, till the shaft is rid
    Close, close beside me keep ;
My eye-lids are together glued,
    And I—and I—must sleep."

" Sleep, brother, sleep, and I will keep
    Close by—heigh-ho !"—To keep
Himself awake the brother strives ;
    But he—he too—must sleep.

" O, mother dear ! wert, wert thou near
    Whilst—sleep !"—The orphan slept ;
And all night long by the black pit-heap
    The mother a dumb watch kept.

And fathers and mothers, and sisters and brothers ;
    The lover and the new-made bride ;
A vigil kept for those who slept,
    From eve to morning tide.

But they slept—still sleep—in silence dread,
　Two hundred old and young,
To awake when heaven and earth have sped,
　And the last dread trumpet rung !

MOTHER WEPT.

MOTHER wept, and father sighed ;
　With delight a-glow
Cried the lad, " to-morrow," cried,
　" To the pit I go."

Up and down the place he sped,
　Greeted old and young,
Far and wide the tidings spread,
　Clapped his hands and sung.

Came his cronies, some to gaze
　Wrapped in wonder ; some
Free with counsel ; some with praise ;
　Some with envy dumb.

" May he," many a gossip cried,
　" Be from peril kept ; "
Father hid his voice and sighed,
　Mother turned and wept.

NANNY TO BESSY.

ELEVEN long winters departed
    Since you and he sailed o'er the main ?
Dear, dear—I've been thrice broken-hearted,
    And thrice—but, ah, let me refrain.—

There was not a lassie in Plessy,
    Nay, truly there was not a lad,
That morning you left us all, Bessy,
    But dropped a kind tear and look'd sad.

A week ere ye went ye were married—
    Yes, yes, I remember aright ;
The lads and the lassies all hurried
    To dance at your bridals that night.

With others, were Mary from Horton,
    And Harry from over the fields ;
Your prim cousin Peggy from Chirton,
    And diddler Allan from Shields.

Piper Tom, with his pipes in the corner,
   Did pipe till the red morn a-broke;
And we danced and we sung in our turn, or
   Gave vent to our glee in a joke.

That seems but last night, tho' eleven
   Black winters have flown since, and yet
Ye're bright as yon star in the heaven,
   Whilst I—but I winnot regret.

Ye're just bright and fresh and as rosy,
   As when ye last left us all, just;
Whilst I am a poor wither'd posy
   The passer has strampt in the dust.

This was not so always; no, clearly
   —When lassies—the burnie has shown
The rose on your dimpled cheek nearly
   Out-matched by the rose on my own.

Nay; as twins we grew up till another
   Was mine—but, another how long?
Then the changes that followed each other,—
   The guilt, and the shame, and the wrong?

R

—Ye knew my 'curst bane and besetter ?
    Brown ? Piers with the thievish black e'e ?
He danced at your wedding, and better
    Than any but Harry danced he.

The sight sent the lasses a-skarling,
    Whenever he came into view ;
And many a fond mother's darling
    Has lived his deception to rue.

Meg Wilson, a-down the green loning,
    Skipped with him a fine afternoon ;
When last she went there she was moaning,
    Her heart like a harp out of tune.

Even Cary, the dour-looking donnet,
    Who'd looked on my downfall with scorn,
Was smit with his blink, and her bonnet
    One Monday was found in the corn.

Nay, many with him tripped and tumbled
    As I'd tripped and tumbled—what then ?
Not one by her fall was so humbled,
    Or put to one half of my pain.

When Harry was brought on a barrow,
    A corpse from the pit, had I known
—But Brown, who had long been his marrow,
    Then, who was so kind as Piers Brown ?

He showed himself ready and willing
    To lighten the load I endured ;
He gather'd me many a shilling,
    And whatso I needed procured.

The bones of my Harry right duly
    Were laid in the grave by his aid ;
Then slipt he to see me—too truly
    So slipt till my pride was low laid.

There's many to point and to titter
    At one who has happen'd a fall—
And into the cup that is bitter,
    The petty still empty their gall.

There's many to point and to titter
    At one that has happen'd to fall—
And into my potion so bitter,
    The petty so emptied their gall.

Then, mine was a hardship and trouble;
  When touched by deceit's magic mace,
My pride went away like a bubble,
  Mine, mine was a pitiful case.

Then mishap to mishap like billow
  To billow succeeded, and I
Was laid with my head on my pillow,
 · And no one to comfort me nigh.

Despised by the world, until riven
  By want were my bairnies from me—
Despised by the world, till mad-driven
  Was I, and mad-driven must be.

Despised by the world, and mad-driven
  Was I, and am fated to be;
There's not under all the blue heaven
  A wofuller woman nor me.

The pale morning finds me a-wringing
  My hands for my jewels in vain;
The day passes by without bringing
  A moment's relief to my pain.

O'ercome by despair in confusion
    Of thought, I will wander oft, when
—Alas, for the charming delusion !—
    They glisten as wont in my ken.

Again on their hazels a-prancing,
    They hie as they hied o'er the way ;
The midges above them a-dancing,
    Are not half so merry as they.

Again up and down the ball boundeth
    Atween their bit hands and the earth,
Till rapture their senses confoundeth,
    And laughter gives vent to their mirth.

Again—"they both live !" my woe banished
    I cry "they both live !" and e'en so,
Awake but to find the birds vanished
    With all that I valued below !

—Nay bann'd from my birth, and attended
    I've been by some devil, and he—
He's laughed when my best dream was ended
    And all that has happen'd to me.

He's dazzled and led me to yammour
For baubles I ought to despise ;
Then whipt from my vision the glamour,
And shown the sad truth to my eyes.

He's mounted the air, and a snelling
Bleak blast's ridden valley and plain ;
And the dwelling of joy made the dwelling
Of dark desolation and pain.—

But let me refrain—since we parted,
Ah, Bessy !—But let me refrain ;
Since then I've been thrice broken-hearted—
But what have I not been since then ?

THE RIDDLE READ.

I THANK my God I ever lived to see the blessed day,
    When the spirit's immortality to me is rendered clear ;
Not by a logic might be made some other tune to play,
    But by a flash of inner light too keen for doubt to bear.

Long, long can death, be death indeed, I asked 'mid doubts
      and fears ;
    Long vainly groped in darkness for the jewels I had lost;
Long listened for an answer to the quest expressed in tears,
    And only found what to the heart a bitterer struggle cost.

Oft in the visions of the night I saw their golden locks,
    I kiss'd their eyes as violets sweet when March with
      boisterous breath,
The lordly oak itself—nay more, the lordly steeple rocks,
    And ever as the morn arose I found them fast in death.

Then said I—If the " be all " and the " end all " of this
      strife,
    Be but to furnish coronals the temples to adorn
Of life's imperious enemy, then, death, and not for life,
    Should be the boon solicited whene'er a babe is born.

Far better man had never been if in a circle he
    Must travel till the little hour of mortal life is ran,
To find when life's dark riddle's read he then must cease
        to be,
    And the end of all his trouble is the end where he began.

To labour in a night on which the sun will never rise—
    To sweat and groan without a hope shall end the bitter
        curse,
Save in a dissolution which shall only close our eyes
    On all we love and cherish—all ?—what destiny were
        worse ?

Not worse were e'en the lot of those the Danaides of yore,
    Condemn'd the hole-fill'd tanks to fill from which the
        waters gushed
As fast as they the fluid in pour'd or could the fluid in
        pour,
    And left them only for their pains a heart by anguish
        crush'd.

Not worse to be like Ixion doom'd on a wheel to spin,
    Transfix'd on which the victim sad arrived at every round,
Just where he did the weary, dizzy, dreary round begin
    Which he—the sore confounded—served the deeper to
        confound.

Not worse to be like Sisyphus, destined up a high hill,
  With many an effort, many a pang still to uproll a rock
Which when the goal was all but won, despite an iron will,
  Re-bounded in a way that made his labours vast, a mock.

Not worse to be like these, for these amid their night of pain
  Had intervals of hope that would the darkest hour illume,
And present loss when viewed aright becomes the future's
    gain,
  And gloom that's past to glory turns to gild the present
    gloom.

But what avails to charm the soul who loves and toils—
    then learns
  That not a vestige of his ME can pass beyond the grave?
That all we love and cherish sink,—when dust to dust
    returns,—
  And with them sink to rise no more the soul in Lethe's
    wave?

In vain to point the past, what can the present yield,
  Except what proves a mock, and still the heart with
    sorrow fills;
And without the charm a future life affords, without a shield
  The soul is left to battle with the worst of human ills.

In vain to point the past, in vain will not its sheen arise
    Upon the mind about to be in death's dark cradle rock'd,
To keener make the thought that when the vital sparklet
       flies,
    Lock'd lies the spirit in the bonds in which the sense is
       lock'd.

To die and be no more is more than we can think, without
    An effort such as rends the heart or petrifies the man :
And when the soul has once began to tread the plain of
       doubt,
    The valley of despair is reached before we halt, or can.

Thus felt I till the truth was found by patient labour sought,
    —By labour and a spirit framed to brook the world's
       harsh scorn ;
When gilded by its sheen a soul was mine with rapture
       fraught,
    And may be yours who seek aright the truths I sought
       to learn.

THE SOUL'S HEREAFTER.

Dies not the soul when dust to dust is given;
    Even as we are in earth-life are we still,
Save from the worn-out garment rent and riven,
    That may have proved a fetter to the will.

Not into demons void of good converted,
    Not into angels void of error—no;
But human-spirited, and human-hearted,
    We on our way with pain or pleasure go.

Not reft of feeling, nay, with feelings keener,
    To other's woes more keen, to others' joys;
With bosoms purer and with minds serener—
    Though human still, more humane we and wise.

Not more to be despised, nor venerated,
    For aught from change of state acquired or caught,
But at our inner value estimated,
    Shall we be shunned or courted as we ought.

Not to their fabled hell, nor fabled heaven,
　　By the good Father's will are we consigned,
But to a sphere of human action—even,
　　To one adapted to each frame and mind.

Not one sweet feeling passeth unrewarded,
　　Not one black deed can go unpunished—not—
Not one swift thought can vanish unrecorded
　　And give no colour to our future lot

Not words but thoughts, and not on faith but actions
　　And on whatever gives our acts their hue,
The heart's allurements, and the minds distractions—
　　Is based the verdict we shall prize or rue.

Yes, such the future that awaits the spirit,
　　Then let us pause and think while pause we can,
How best we may the meed eternal merit,
　　That shall be to the weal eterne of man.

THE HELL BROTH.

THE devil and the devil's brood
  Around a boiling caldron hung,
While in a nook in merry mood
  Grim Death a dainty ditty sung ;
For guided by a baleful star
  The devil himself had caused to beam,
Lo, myriads hurried from afar
  To reap the fruit of a darksome dream :
On, on they came with cheek a-flame,
  And lips that quivered as they sought
In tones subdued the demon brood,
  For but a drop of the magic pot.
—Anon around was the hell-broth spun,
  And a measure brimmed to old and young,
The while delighted with the fun,
  Grim Death a dainty ditty sung.

That potion quaft, in his conceit
  Behold the dwarf a giant tread,
At least a hundred thousand feet
  Above his worthier neighbour's head ;
Despising still or lord or serf,
  About the land he strutting goes,
'Till bang against a brother dwarf,
  The merry fellow runs his nose :—
Thus many a one—loon, fop, and clown—
  A lesson to their sorrow got,
And yet aloud they pray the brood
  For deeper draughts of the magic pot.
—Anon around was the hell-broth spun,
  And a measure drained by old and young,
The while delighted with the fun,
  Grim Death a dainty ditty sung.

Now double-drugg'd the rout about
  A soul-consuming furnace bore,
And what they took to put it out,
  But only made it burn the more :
It burnt in heart, it burnt in brain,
  And from its fumes arose a sprite,
One, whom her favours to obtain
  They chased by day, they chased by night ;

And still as they deemed her their prey,
 Away, away with a leer she shot,
'Mid cries right loud to the demon brood,
 For deeper draughts of the magic pot.
—Again around was the hell-broth spun,
 And a measure drained by old and young,
The while delighted with the fun,
 Grim Death a daintier ditty sung.

So la, ta, la !—that fiery draught
 Now led them one and all a dance :
Lo, ere the drug was wholly quaft,
 Each threw on each a lurid glance ;
And from that glance a wasp took wing,
 From busy tongue to ear it flew,
And ever around it bore a sting
 The devil himself had cause to rue :
It stung them black, it stung them blue,
 And with each sting the louder got
Their cries right loud to the demon brood,
 For deeper draughts of the magic pot.
—Again around was the hell-broth spun,
 And a measure drained by old and young,
The while delighted with the fun,
 Grim Death a daintier ditty sung.

That horrid draught being duly quaft,
   A cry o'er plain and mountain rolled,
At which the strong the weaker took,
   And bartered body and soul for gold :
And of the gold thus gotten they
   At once a gloomy castle built
Whose dome might from the eye of day
   Forever hide their horrid guilt :
Tombed in their victims' blood-price thus,
   Long revelled they and faltered not
To cry aloud to the demon brood,
   For deeper draughts of the magic pot.
—But around no more was the hell-broth spun ;
   Awe-struck the fiends in the pot had sprung,
The while surfeited with the fun,
   Death cursed the dainty lay he'd sung.

THE REIGN OF GOLD.

IT sounded in castle and palace,
    It sounded in cottage and shed,
It sped over mountains and valleys,
    And withered the earth as it sped;
Like a blast in its fell consummation
    Of all that we holy should hold,
Thrilled, thrilled thro' the nerves of the nation,
    A cry for the reign of King Gold.

Upstarted the chiefs of the city,
    And sending it back with a ring,
To the air of a popular ditty,
    Erected a throne to the king;
'Twas based upon fiendish persuasions,
    Cemented by crimes manifold:
Embellished by specious ovations,
    That dazzled the foes of King Gold.

T

The prey of unruly emotion,
  The miner and diver go forth,
And the depths of the earth and the ocean
  Are shorn of their lustre and worth ;
The mountain is riven asunder,
  The days of the valley are told ;
And sinew, and glory, and grandeur,
  Are sapped for a smile of King Gold.

Beguiled of their native demeanour,
  The high rush with heirlooms and bays,
The poor with with what gold cannot weigh, nor
  The skill of the pedant appraise ;
The soldier he spurs with his duty,
  And lo ! by the frenzy made bold,
The damsel she glides with her beauty,
  To garnish the brow of King Gold.

Accustomed to traffic forbidden
  By honour—by heaven—each hour,
The purest, by conscience unchidden,
  Laugh, laugh at the noble and pure :
And Chastity, rein'd in halter,
  Is led to the temple and sold,—
Devotion herself, at the altar,
  Yields homage alone to King Gold.

Affection on whose honey blossom,
  The child of affliction still fed—
Affection is plucked from the bosom,
  And malice implanted instead;
And dark grow the brows of the tender,
  And colder the hearts of the cold :—
Love, pity, and justice surrender
  Their charge of the hounds of King Gold.

See, see, from the sear'd earth ascending,
  A cloud o'er the welkin expands ;
See, see, 'mid the dense vapour bending,
  Pale women with uplifted hands ;
Smokes thus to the bridegroom of Circe,
  The dear blood of hundreds untold ;
Invoke thus the angel of mercy,
  A curse on the reign of King Gold.

It sounded in castle and palace,
  It sounded in cottage and shed,
It sped over mountains and valleys,
  And withered the earth as it sped ;
Like a blast in its fell consummation,
  Of all that we holy should hold,
Thrilled, thrilled thro' the nerves of the Nation ;
  "Cling ! Clang ! for the reign of King Gold."

THE DOWNFALL OF MAMMON.

THE baleful Era of King Gold is vanished,
    And men disgusted with the part they played,
From out the temple of the heart are banished
    The idols that debased the soul they swayed.

Man yet has passions and the cause of passions,
    And so will have in his best future state;
But he has reason too by which he fashions
    Them into servants for a purpose great.

Instead of selfhood and of actions cruel,
    Inspired by love heroic deeds abound,
And charity's esteemed a richer jewel
    Than ever yet in Orient mine was found.

Instead of servitude and evil doing,
    Inspired by freedom men erected wear
Their sun-crowned brows and a high course pursuing,
    Whatever they deem right to do, they dare.

Instead of falsehood, truth their speech inspireth—
    Inspires their thoughts and permeates the man,
Till spoken promises a worth acquireth,
    Which merely written missives never can.

Instead of superstition grim and hideous,
    Religion triumphs ; and whate'er obtains,
No longer envy can with hints invidious
    Cause man to visit brother man with pain.

Thus in ways manifold, sublime and glorious,
    The God-sprung tenants of the earth at last
Arise o'er every " mortal ill victorious,"
    That made their life a hell-life in the past.

No longer prompted by fell aspirations,
    Does man send havoc into realms afar,
But gains from acts of peace more prized ovations
    Than ever gratified the sons of war.

No longer to his inner part disloyal,
    He learneth from the " still small voice " he scorned
How to become a king in act, more royal
    Than ever yet a throne of gold adorned.

No longer bound to themes abhorred or hated,
   On highest subjects is the mind employed;
And as by war no land is desolated,
   From lack of love no heart is left a void.

By cords of sympathy, before the altar,
   Not chains of gold are youth and virgin drawn;
And when the trite " I will" their accents falter,
   It's falter'd from two hearts by bliss o'er-flown.

No want of union, and no fatal duel,
   Fought by two hearts in silence grim, if not,
In cruel actions or in words as cruel,
   The lot of wedlock makes a bitter lot.

A circle round the hearthstone, young and olden,
   The family gather, and their feelings blend
And inter-blend till in a concord golden,
   As one they labour for some common end.

In time those circles form but inner circles
   To circles greater, till the nations act
As one vast soul whose sphere with glory sparkles,
   And heaven the dream on earth is heaven the fact.

Onward and upward move the nations, onward
    And ever upward thus the earth-born move—
Till like the gilded fanes that pointed sun-ward,
    Their soul-flames touch the souls of those above.

Then in a way hard to be comprehended,
    As hills are cleft were hills ere time began,
So are the barriers asunder rended
    That kept apart the angel and the man.

Illumined by a light celestial, even
    To them the life beyond the Veil's unfurl'd ;
And messages of import sweet are given
    Unto the outer from the inner world.

Not dead are found the jewels death had captured—
    Not, tho' their dust be scattered by the wind ;
Not dead, but living, and with hearts enraptured,
    Still toiling for the dear ones left behind.

United soul to loving soul, united
    Blent heaven and earth in one harmonic whole—
" Glory to God " shout one and all delighted,
    And " Hallelujah " rings from pole to pole.

The baleful Era of King Gold has vanished—
   The idols that debased the soul they chained,
From out the temple of the heart are banished,
   And the millenium's at length obtained.

THE SEATON TERRACE LASS :

A BALLAD.

My love at Seaton Terrace dwells,
   A hale and hearty wight,
Who lilts away the summer day,
   Also the winter night :
The merriest bird with rapture stirr'd,
   Could never yet surpass
The melody awaken'd by
   The Seaton Terrace lass !

She's graceful as a lily-wand,
　Right modest too is she,
And then ye'll search in vain the land
　To find a busier bee ;
Like silver clear her iron gear
　Like burnished gold, the brass—
For tidyness there's none to peer
　The Seaton Terrace lass.

More restless than a clucking hen
　About her, Minnie stirs ;
" Go, jewel, knit your fancy net,
　And I will scour the floors."
" Enjoy the day, a-down the way,
　Where greenest grows the grass,
No help I need," replies with speed
　The Seaton Terrace lass.

She'll knit or sew, she'll bake or brew—
　She'll wash the clothes so clean,
The very daisy pales beside
　Her linen on the green ;
Then what she'll do, with ease she'll do,
　And still her manner has
A charm, would gar a stoic woo
　The Seaton Terrace lass.

U

Discomfort flies her dark-brown eyes,
  And when the men folk come
All black and weary from the pit,
  They find a welcome home.
Her brothers tease her, and a pride,
  The father feeleth as
Again he meets again he greets
  The Seaton Terrace lass.

When day is past and night at last
  Begins to cloud the dell,
She'll take her skiel and out she'll steal,
  And meet me at the well ;
Then, oh ! how fleet the moments sweet—
  Yet fleeter shall they pass,
That night the Bebside laddie weds
  The Seaton Terrace lass.

THE COLLIER LAD :

A BALLAD.

MY lad he is a Collier Lad,
   And a blithe, blithe soul is he,
And when a holiday comes round,
   He'll spend that day in glee :
He'll tell his tale o'er a pint o' ale,
   And crack his joke, and bad
Must be the heart who loveth not
   To hear the Collier Lad.

At bowling matches on the green
   He ever takes the lead,
For none can swing his arm and fling
   With such a pith and speed ;
His bowl is seen to skim the green,
   And bound as it were glad,
To hear the cry o' victory
   Salute the Collier Lad.

When 'gainst the wall they play the ball,
    He's never known to lag,
But up and down he gars it bowne,
    Till all his rivals fag ;
When deftly,—lo ! he strikes a blow
    Which gars them all look sad,
And wonder how it came to pass
    They play'd the Collier Lad.

The quoits are out, the hobs are fix'd,
    The first round quoit he flings
Enrings the hob ; and lo ! the next
    The hob again unrings ;
And thus he'll play a summer's day,
    The theme o' those who gad ;
And youngsters shrink to bet their brass
    Against the Collier Lad.

When in the dance he doth advance,
    The rest all sigh to see
How he can spring and kick his heels,
    When they a-wearied be ;
Your one-two-three, with either knee
    He'll beat, and then, glee mad,
A summerset will crown the dance,
    Danced by the Collier Lad.

Besides a will and pith and skill,
  My laddie owns a heart
That never once would suffer him
  To act a cruel part ;
That to the poor would ope the door
  To share the last he had ;
And many a secret blessing's pour'd
  Upon my Collier Lad.

He seldom goes to church, I own,
  And when he does, why then,
He with a leer will sit and hear,
  And doubt the holy men ;
This very much annoys my heart,
  But soon as we are wed,
To please the priest, I'll do my best
  To tame my Collier Lad.

THE UNFORGOTTEN ONE.

I.

Too lovely art thou to behold,
　　And not to be stung by desire,
To bathe in those ringlets of gold,
　　To bathe in those glances of fire.

Too lovely art thou to the ken,
　　And twenty times so unto mine,
Since all the desires are in vain,
　　With which I am destined to pine :

Not that but I'm agile and young,
　　And exult in the strength of an arm,
Could shield thee from every wrong,
　　Could shield thee from every harm :

Not that with a heart-chilling pride,
　　Thou would'st hark to my ardent appeal ;
Not that thou would'st seek to deride,
　　What thus I am fated to feel.

No, no—for upon thy fair brow
   Is the stamp of a heart meek and kind ;
And however thy beauty may glow,
   It but adds to the charms of thy mind :

'Tis that while the fates have combined
   With nature to bless thee, too drear
The lot to thy lover assigned
   For aught but the wretched to share.

II.

I saw but once that lovely one.
   Nor need I see her twice to love ;
She broke upon me like the dawn,
   And o'er my soul her magic wove—
Yea, forced the lion stern to own
   Himself the captive of the dove.

She brought the morn, she left the night ;
   Nor strove I to throw off the chain :
But rather felt a sweet delight
   To intermingle with the pain
That made my heart's repose a blight,
   Till madness ruled my thought's domain.

By night I sought a solitude,
　And gave unto the winds a grief
That struggled like the lava flood,
　That boils and struggles for relief ;
And night still left me in a mood
　Unto the voice of reason deaf.

The radiant planets in their flight,
　And she the quiet Queen of heaven,
With glory garmented the night ;
　But not to them the power was given
To kill, but rather nurse the blight
　By which afar my peace was driven.

Yet wished I not the sun to rise,
　For then the world were up, and then
Were I exposed to wistful eyes,
　And questions bold of forward men,
Who deem themselves both good and wise,
　Yet neither know nor pity pain.

And what on earth—ay, what in hell
　Can be more racking to the thought,
Than that our pangs unspeakable
　Should, disregarded, be as nought ;
Or look'd upon with looks that tell
　In vain would sympathy be sought ?

The magic vision fled, and so
  Have all those precious feelings, all !
Which gave to life a golden glow—
  Which made a joy this earthly ball—
And now, what's left to me ? what, oh !
  What, but a cup of very gall ?

III.

Oh, chaunt that theme again, sweet girl !
  That theme enchanting more, to me,
Than ocean's richest, purest pearl,
  To miser's heart could ever be.

Thy lay's the language of a heart
  By blighted hopes delirious grown,
And mine has felt as keen a smart
  As e'er to beauty's dupe was known.

It tells of tears that flowed unseen,--
  Of sighs that woke and died unheard,—
Such, such, sweet girl, my lot has been,
  And such too oft is faith's reward.

V

'Tis something still to know, alone
    I have not trod the path of grief ;
And joining in another's moan.
        Will give the bursting heart relief.

Then, chaunt that theme, sweet girl, again.
    That theme so sweet, so sad to me ;
And I w'!! join the pensive strain,
    And mourn the lover's lot with thee.

THE GUARDIAN ANGEL.

I'M the spirit Emmalina thy guardian angel, and
Drawn hither by a subtle law but few can understand—
The golden cord of sympathy I leave the summer-land
    Thy aching brows with lilies to entwine.

I have watched thee late and early, I have watched thee on
        the morn ;
And when the sun has left the sky and Luna like a lorn
Dejected maid has brought the hour most prized by hearts,
        grief-torn,
    I thy aching brows with lilies have entwined.

I have watched thee in the battle with the many ills of life,

And then when sleep has seized thee only to renew the
strife

In dreams has made thy woe too rife appear more keen and
rife,

I thy aching brows with lilies have entwined.

I have watched when dark and dreary has been thy horo-
scope,

And when thou strength has needed most with cark and
care to cope,

I have nerved thy arm, into thy heart have pour'd the oil
of hope—

I thy aching brows with lilies have entwined.

BEHIND THE VEIL :

A PSYCHIC CHAUNT.

"A PHANTOM to me thou appearest,
    But spite of this seeming I know
The magical image thou wearest,
    Is real as the lilies in blow ;
As real and as rare as the fairest of all our fair lilies in blow.

"Not alive to the senses external,
    Of hearing, the touch, or the sight—
Not aught that would yield to the carnal
    Desire a delusive delight ;
But alive to the spirit eternal art thou, and its joy day and
    night.

"Not alive to the outer but inner
    Keen sense of the spirit, and when
I'm far from the world and its din, or
    Low chat of most women and men,
I see in thy form what no artist could portray with pencil
    or pen.

"Not a phantom so call'd, but a glory—
  An outburst of sheen from the sky,
At which the black evils before thee
  Upheave their huge pinions and fly—
At which I too mantled in glory am borne to the regions
    on high.

"Uplifted on raptures bright pinions,
  I tread the bright zones of the blest;
I enter the azure dominions
  Of those who have long been at rest
From the turmoil, the strife, the opinions by which here the
    good are opprest.

"Away o'er the gold-crested mountains
  I hie light of foot as the roe;
I drink of the pellucid fountains
  That flow in the valleys below,
And that instant both valleys and mountains with a deeper
    significance glow.

"Yea, awake to the meaning and grandeur
  By which I'm surrounded, I gaze;
And gazing thus wonder on wonder
  The disenthrall'd spirit surveys;
And I see that on which I may ponder but never reveal in
    those days.

" Ah me, what availeth the vision
    Of music-soul'd bard, seer, or sage ;
When bigotry, self, superstition
    Unite their fell forces to wage
A war upon truth and its mission, when learning would
    fetter the age ?

" What, what would it be to the nations
    Did I give what I'd give for love's sake ?
Would they hearken the blest revelations
    I'd deem it my duty to make ?
They'd say I had drank of libations should doom me to
    dungeon or stake.

" Yet freely the truth should be spoken
    Could I but unfold it and say
How when from its manacles broken,
    The soul to the spheres wings away,
We find where we go not a token of what our paid bishops
    portray.

" This learn we in joy—ay, or sadness—
    For tho' be the creeds, new and old,
The offspring of falsehood and madness,
    The scrolls of the past are unroll'd,
And we see as if shown in a mirror each fact there is there
    to unfold.

" On all can be seen by the spirit,
    Around us, above us, below ;
Nay, even the homes we inherit,
    Are graced or defaced—gloom or glow,
With merit our merit, demerit, our shame and joy, glory
        and woe.

" Not in dead pictures merely but living
    Bright symbols our deeds speak and move :
And we see with the gifts we have given
    In the God-enshrined spirit of love,
The lest of our sins tho' forgiven can never be cancelled
        above.

" Hence we gather the unborn hereafter,
    From out the live present is born :
That the laugher is stripped of his laughter,
    The mask from the masker is torn :
The crafty is whipt by his craft and the scorner is met by
        his scorn.

"This learn we, but learn too, whatever
    The strength and the hue of our creed,
That a good deed's a good deed and never
    Can other be than a good deed ;
That destiny's self cannot sever nor keep from the worthy
        his need.

" To the disenthrall'd spirit is granted

All this, and things deeper to know,

That in numbers of fire should be chaunted

To creed ridden mortals below,

Could the feelings by which I am haunted be taught in

bright numbers to flow.

" But of this I despair; and I wander

With one once a mortal to find

The marvels we see and their grandeur

Can never be shown to mankind,

Till each for himself's learned to ponder and feel the sad

fact he is blind."

THE VITAL SPARK :

AN INNER VOICE.

BEWILDERED by Life's Gordian Knot long o'er me
　　Despair had flung her adamantine chain,
When thro' the abyss of my spirit " Glory !"
　　A deep voice cried, and "Glory !" then this strain :—

" A spark eternal from the co-eternal
　　And inner source of light ere time began,
The soul built from the dust its home external,
　　And so became what we now know as man.

" The outer temple built, an inner, finer
　　From this and like to this was next ordained,
In which might be attained a life diviner
　　Than could within the outer be attained.
　　　　　　　W

" Thus in the image in man's form reflected,
  From out the universal soul the soul
Its individuality projected,
  And so became a whole within the whole.

" From root and knot, from knot and leaf to blossom,
  Upsprang by slow degrees the oak to view :
So by degrees as slow from out God's bosom,
  The vital spark to man immortal grew.

" As by degrees he thus obtained his being,
  So by degrees his mental prime's obtained
When grown from man the blind to man the seeing,
  The chains are rent in twain by which he's chained.

" Then from the chaos of the days primeval,
  Into the future far his ken extends—
Then to his ken what error seemed and evil
  Appear but instruments to noble ends.

" The shadow's self thus seen becomes a splendour,
  The mystic maze pervaded by a plan :
And laws sublime to intersect and render
  Harmonic what but discord seemed to man.

" In matter's seen the means to vanquish matter,
    In many a dismal ban a blessing bright;
In states chaotic what their gloom might scatter,
    And their domains enshrine in living light.

" The darkest woe the brightest joy enclaspeth,
    In what seems false is seen the true, a power
Which grasped by man as rich a mace he graspeth,
    As ever graced the mythic gods of yore.

" A thinker clear nor less a doer ; even
    A more than soul Titanic he, who still
Can make the very death-forged bolts of heaven
    To dance attendance on his potent will.

" The very lightning that the vision dazzles,
    The very tempest that the forest rends,
Are vassals bound unto his will, and vassals
    That help to realize the highest ends.

" Even as he wills empires arise—inventions
    Are seen uniting foreign land to land ;
And where but winds and waves held dire contentions,
    By sweetest intercourse the deeps are spann'd.

" A victor o'er the elements, a victor
   E'en over self he moves till lo, appears
Upon the earth he treads the very picture
   Of what can be in the seraphic spheres.

" From higher than the seraph state descended,
   Up to the goal from whence he came he climbs ;
And when the days of mortal life are ended,
   Still upward scales he thro' long future times.

" Just as the bee with honey laden flieth,
   To hive the guerdon earned by toil and pang ;
So by experience enriched, he hieth
   With power to gift the Power from whom he sprang.

" Yea, ever moves he glory-ward, and ever
   Does glory to the Love Eterne accord !"
Thus rang that voice within my soul, and never
   Shall I forget how sweet the voice thus heard.

THE ANGEL AND THE SEER.

" I HAVE oped thy inner vision,"
   (Spake the Spirit to the Seer,)
" Now I'll show to thee the mission
   Which whate'er betides—whate'er—
Thou by heaven's high permission shalt accomplish.—Give
     ear !

" Thou shalt write and speak and wholly
   By the gift of speech and song,
Thou shalt make the proud one lowly,
   And the weak in spirit, strong,
And the servitor of folly for the ways of wisdom long.

" Thou shalt teach he who devises
   Harm for others, harm will meet,
And that he who most despises
   Counsel's—to himself a cheat ;
That the wisest of the wise is most devoid of self-conceit.

" Thou shalt speak a word in season
  To the poor in bondage, nor
Forget to say 'tis treason
  'Ganst the highest to ignore
The claims of love and reason and to trample on the
  poor.

.

" Thou shalt teach the tyrant master
  How to view his servants lot ;
Not to want the wheels go faster
  Then there's strength to do it—not—
Not to make it a disaster to be cradled in a cot.

" Thou shalt teach the willing toiler
  Doomed for fee to shape and plan,
He has that which no dispoiler
  May divest him of—nor can—
The power to make his scorner feel the dignity of man.

" Thou shalt tell the sordid miser
  Not heaps of guinea gold
Will ever make him wiser—
  For wisdom ne'er was sold,
And lacking which his joys are too meagre to be told.

" Ask what will be his measure
　　When dust to dust's restored ;
What shall serve his gold, what pleasure
　　Shall gems the soul afford ?
And if his worshipped treasure shall be worth one tender.
　　word.

" Are the deeds encircling
　　The heart enshrined in love—
The brightest jewels sparkling
　　In the courts above,
And lacking which we darkling down to our soul sphere
　　move.

" All this in words unvarnished
　　Say to the world ; and say,
That lives by deeds ungarnished
　　Must be deplored—and may
As much as lives crime-tarnished which other traits display.

" Strike, strike at superstition,
　　Bid its slaves with open eyes,
See in lack of a volition
　　For themselves to think, there lies
A more damnable perdition than the bigots can devise.

" Bid each for himself but ponder,
　　And e'en though he err persist ;
And the fetters he will sunder,
　　That now threaten to resist ;
Nay, o'er long he'll come to wonder how so long he lay in
　　　　mist.

" Risen on the wings of rapture,
　　At his freedom he will soar
Far 'yond the reach of Scripture
　　Misconstruers evermore
To redazzle, to recapture by their guile engendered lore.

" Leaving churches and their minions,
　　Leaving books and bells and beads,
Leaving craftdom's dark dominions
　　To the bigots and their creeds,
He will stamp his bold opinions on the coin of golden
　　　　deeds.

" Thus thy thought shall like a sabre
　　Cut some knot, if not untie,
And some duty to a neighbour
　　Do—and yet a nobler—ay,
A higher, holier labour must thy efforts yet employ.

"See, you desolated woman
  Weeping o'er an infant lost;
Tearing out her hair, consuming
  Life in anguish, till a ghost
She seems and not a woman weeping o'er her baby lost.

"Go, take her hand extended—
  In words of music say,
How the spirit that descended
  Once on Pentecost, yet may
The bosom heal thus rended — say the child's not far
    away.

"Say, In fact the little jewel
  Not a clod sepulchred lies—
Ah, the cruel creed, the cruel
  Hearts can teach such creed unwise !
That her jewel, yet a jewel will sparkle in her eyes.

"Aloud let it be sounded
  Whoever were, yet are ;
Not lost in space unbounded,
  Not in another star—
That yet around, about us are the friends we deem
    afar.

" This may sound like a gigantic
　　Fiction to the world—'tis true,
And thou be held an antic,
　　And bigots not a few
Will with a fairy frantic thy lonely steps pursue.

" Slander black, and black detraction,—
　　All the poison'd darts of hate,
All the malice of a faction
　　Whose wounded pride would sate
Itself on thy distraction to brook shall be thy fate.

" But thou shalt stand undaunted,
　　The arrows at thee hurl'd,
Till on falsehood's grave implanted
　　The flag of truth's unfurl'd,
And a mighty pean's chanted by her angels to the world.

" That shall be a day of glory—
　　Glory to our God on high—
Glory to the angels o'er ye—
　　Glory and exceeding joy—
Glory to the nations—glory to the seer they'd now de-
　　stroy.

" Thus I've oped thy inner vision

In the language of thy kind

Have shown to thee the mission

For which thou art designed—

Then go and with God's blessing do the work to thee

assigned."

NOTE.

THE RING, page 71. There is a tradition that Essex had elicited from Queen Elizabeth a ring as a token of confidence, with the assurance that if ever he should incur her displeasure, or need her assistance, by the production of the said ring she should be pacified, or that assistance given. Afterwards the Earl was impeached for high treason, tried, and condemned, when to the last the Queen anxiously awaited the forthcoming of the token which should have secured his pardon. The talisman did not come, and the Earl was executed. Years after, the Queen discovered that the Earl had, by a confidant sent to her the ring, but that from malicious motives it had not been delivered, whereat she went nearly frantic, and died a few days after of a broken heart.

THE END.

George Richardson, Printer, Bedlington.